A Question of Loyalty

A
Question of
Loyalty

PAUL M. SNIDERMAN

University of California Press
Berkeley • Los Angeles • London

University of California Press
Berkeley and Los Angeles, California

University of California Press, Ltd.
London, England

© 1981 by
The Regents of the University of California
Printed in the United States of America

1 2 3 4 5 6 7 8 9

Library of Congress Cataloging in Publication Data

Sniderman, Paul M
  A question of loyalty.

  Includes index.
  1. Political participation—United States—Public
opinion. 2. Allegiance—United States—Public
opinion. 3. Alienation (Social psychology)—
Public opinion. 4. Public opinion—United States.
5. Personality and Politics. I. Title.
JK1764.S57   323'.042'0973   80-22932
ISBN 0-520-04196-8
ISBN 0-520-04413-4 (ppr.)

To Mark and Jennifer
and all the parents
of their parents

Contents

Preface

The Social Indicators Project was the beginning. It included Charles Glock and Richard Ofshe; Gertrude Selznick and Karen Paige; Arthur Stinchcombe and William Nichols; Herbert McClosky, Jack Citrin, J. Merrill Shanks—overall principal investigator—and myself. Prejudice was the interest of the first two, the status of women that of the second two, methodology that of the third two, political alienation that of the last four. A history of a research program consisting of ten investigators would have to be written, I suspect, by an eleventh. For my part I have benefited from my collaborators in the overall project; but the alienation section of it was the center for me. It was a collaborative effort. We hammered out the details of the study together, with each of my colleagues heading up, from time to time, planning and administration. However each of them may judge his contribution, I have profited greatly from all of them.

This book got its real start some years after the larger project was underway. There was something about the notion of developing a social indicator of alienation as we were pledged to do that troubled me. Herbert McClosky, after studying a sketch of some of my notions, encouraged me to pin them down empirically and fought for the research support to allow me to do just that.

I have been fortunate in terms of support. The National Science Foundation (NSF Grant Number SOC72-05214

A03) sponsored the original project—Jack Citrin, Richard Gunther, Merrill Shanks and Herbert McClosky are preparing the report. A grant from the Russell Sage Foundation and a Guggenheim Fellowship underwrote the empirical analysis for this book. A year at the Center for Advanced Study in the Behavioral Sciences saw me through the first draft, not a small accomplishment when being distracted by one of the happiest of years. I also want to thank the *British Journal of Political Science* for permission to make use of my article "The Politics of Faith," which is the basis of Chapter Two.

I have had a number of colleagues in this effort: they have shared with me their conviction that what I was doing was worth doing; and they have been generous in criticism. I hesitate to single out my fellow fellows at the Center but I am so very grateful to Houston Baker, Sacvan Bercovitch, Mary Bogdonoff, Michael Hannan, Anthony King and Ted Lowi. Grant Barnes and Sheila Levine got me through patches when this book was not writable. It would also be difficult to exaggerate the help of Robert Axelrod, Charles L. Bann, Richard Brody, David Elkins, Cynthia Warias, and, above all, Barbara and Raymond Wolfinger.

Then there is Susan.

1

Introduction

Many Americans no longer believe that their government can be trusted to do what is right; or that it is run for their benefit; or that the people running it know what they are doing. And it is not just politics that has disillusioned them. The leadership of nearly every key institution of America—including medicine, higher education, organized religion, the military, the Supreme Court—has suffered a severe loss of public confidence. This loss, many feel, is symptomatic of a broader malady. Accounts vary; but the warning signs include the disaffection of citizens and the rise of adversary politics. We face, they say, a crisis of confidence.[1]

Perhaps. But to know how citizens feel about government—to know more are alienated or fewer allegiant—is not enough. The quality of their judgment matters, too. What is decisive, I think, is the readiness to recognize that

1. Arthur Miller, "Political Issues and Trust in Government," *American Political Science Review* 68 (1974): 951-972, especially table 1, p. 953. For a cautionary criticism see Jack Citrin, "Comment," ibid., pp. 973-988. For a judicious review of the evidence see Everett Ladd, "The Polls: The Question of Confidence," *Public Opinion Quarterly*, Winter 1976/77, pp. 544-552. For recent statements of opposing interpretations on the validity of a "crisis of confidence" see Patrick H. Caddell, "Crisis of Confidence I—Trapped in a Downward Spiral," *Public Opinion* 2 (October/November 1979), and Warren E. Miller, "Crisis of Confidence II—Misreading the Public Pulse," ibid., pp. 9-15. For more general interpretations see Robert Nisbet, *Twilight of Authority* (New York: Oxford University Press, 1975); Jurgen Habermas, "Legitimation Problems in Late Capitalism," *Social Research* 40 (Winter 1973): 643-667; Daniel Bell, *The Cultural Contradictions of Capitalism* (New York: Basic Books, 1978); Samuel P. Huntington, "The United States," in Michael J. Crozier, Samuel P. Huntington and Jori Watanuki, *The Crisis of Democracy* (New York: New York University Press, 1975).

this system of government, for all its virtues, has its faults
—and the other way about. Some citizens are ready to
acknowledge there is something to be said on the other
side; their judgment is more evenhanded, more differentiated—in a word, more balanced.

Judgment of Government

Being alienated or allegiant is one thing; having a balanced judgment is another. A citizen may dislike government—he may be bitterly critical of it—without losing
perspective or balance. Or he may think highly of it, and
lack balance. And unless we pay attention to whether
citizens' judgment of government is balanced—and not
just whether they are alienated or allegiant—we are likely
to mistake the habits of mind that favor democratic
politics.

It is tempting to take the change in public attitudes
toward political institutions as evidence of healthy skepticism.[2] The politics of the last two decades, in this view,
have been a hard taskmaster: they have taught many
citizens that public officials will get things wrong sooner
or later; that when things go wrong it is a citizen's right,
and arguably his duty, to express his complaints and to
act on his criticisms; and, finally, that a distrust of leaders
can be a salutary part of the practice as well as of the
theory of democratic government.

A sanguine view. But how many citizens see that it is
precisely because leaders may be untrustworthy that the
institutions of representative democracy are designed to
set one off against the other? How many have a new
appreciation of checks and balances, or of the separation

2. Vivien Hart, *Distrust and Democracy* (Cambridge: Cambridge University Press, 1978).

of powers, or of judicial review? It is the institutions of liberal democracy—not just unpopular leaders or shady practices—which are the target of public criticism. And their failings seem confounded with their virtues. Liberal institutions have not won special praise for restraining elites; and they have come under fire for frustrating citizens—for not being responsive or really representative. Cynicism is not the same thing as skepticism. The mood of disillusion which has settled over the country is disquieting. Yet as we may be too quick to welcome popular support for public institutions, we may be too ready to worry about its loss. What would we have thought, one might ask, if citizens had not become more cynical? The last two decades have seen political scandal, assassination, riot, war, Watergate. If citizens could have watched this parade of horrors without having their confidence disturbed, they would have proven themselves incapable of judgment, and we should have had to abandon the idea of citizenship.

There is cause for concern: a citizen who is overready to disapprove of government may be overready to contest it, or refuse to comply with it. Whether a person is indeed overready to disapprove of government may be the decisive aspect of his orientation toward government. Two people may be equally alienated, yet the judgment of one may be comparatively evenhanded, that of the other plainly onesided. And just as the allegiant may not suit the temper of a democratic politics if they lack balance, the alienated may not threaten it if they have balance.

I do not mean to suggest that a balanced judgment is all that is important, or imply that others, in not focusing on it, have looked at what is unimportant. They have concentrated, rightly, on comparing the alienated and the allegiant to learn the causes and consequences of the public's loss of confidence in political authorities. They have

worked at defining and measuring key terms—at honing
distinctions between general and specific support, responsiveness, legitimacy, alienation, cynicism.[3] By contrast, I
shall use words like *alienated* and *cynical* more or less
interchangeably, not because a distinction between them
cannot be drawn but because drawing it would only tend
to obscure the distinction that matters most to me—
whether a citizen's judgment of government is balanced
or not.

Of course, a word like alienation is abstract, complex,
ambiguous. But no more so than a hundred other ones.
Indeed, far from its meaning being peculiarly elusive,
there is substantial agreement on what is indicative or
diagnostic of being politically alienated—a state of affairs
which tends to be chiefly obscured by paying attention to
what researchers *say* they do rather than to what they in
fact do. As a practical matter I take alienation to mean
what they also take it to mean: specifically, the more
unfavorable citizens' attitudes are toward the political
order, the more cynical, disaffected, alienated they are;
conversely, the more favorable their attitudes, the more
trusting, supportive, allegiant they are.

There is no shortage of distinctions to make. One can
argue that the notion of alienation consists of a number
of distinct dimensions such as legitimacy and responsiveness. Or one can argue that how citizens feel about the
political system must be distinguished with precision from
how they feel about incumbent leaders. I happen to be of
the opinion that these particular distinctions are rather
less obvious than one might at first think.[4] But the test of

3. For one of the clearest and most current expositions see David Easton,
"A Re-assessment of the Concept of Political Support," *British Journal of
Political Science* 5 (October 1975): 435-458.
4. See Appendix A,"A Note on the Measurement of Political Alienation."

a distinction is whether it is profitable, not whether it is arguable. And for my purposes the distinction to emphasize is between those whose judgment of government is balanced and those whose judgment is not, and this quite apart from whether they are alienated or they are allegiant. Alienation is not, at bottom, my subject; but the turmoil of the last two decades does allow me to take up an older question: Which habits of mind are congenial, and which inimical, to a democratic politics?

The Design of the Study

The mission of the larger study, of which this book is one aspect, is the development of social indicators in three areas—prejudice, the status of women and political alienation. For all the differences among them, the three share a common aim: to devise dependable indicators of change, based not on objective measures (for example, the rate of inflation) but on individual reports of subjective states. This aim dominates the study design.[5]

We shared interests and, to a lesser extent, problems. So the three areas took the first step in concert—conducting a survey of the adult population of the five-county San Francisco Bay Area. The questionnaire was a collaborative effort. The participants in each of the three groups took responsibility for developing a battery of questions for their own area of interest and expertise. The hour-long interview, consequently, was divided into four nearly equal parts—sections on alienation, prejudice, the status of women and miscellaneous matters of interest to all, such as education or occupation.

With the assistance of the field staff of the Survey Re-

5. The objective was common, but the strategies were, properly, various; here I shall report only the alienation aspect of the larger project.

search Center, Berkeley, we drew a full probability cluster sample of the adult population of the San Francisco-Oakland Standard Metropolitan Statistical Area. This five-county area (Alameda, Contra Costa, Marin, San Francisco and San Mateo) had a population of slightly more than three million in 1970. We interviewed 963 of these people in the summer of 1972. This sample I shall call the Bay Area Survey (BAS).[6]

The BAS sample is uncommon in one respect: it includes, by design, more blacks than would be interviewed in a strict probability sample. (Since prejudice was the prime interest of one group of researchers, the reasons for this are obvious and compelling.) But everything has a price. To increase the number of black ghetto respondents we had to decrease the number of non-black respondents who would otherwise have been interviewed. A weighting factor, calculated in the customary fashion, has been introduced to correct for this special feature of the sample. The unweighted number of respondents is 963; the weighted N is 1,000.

Beyond the BAS each area pursued a separate strategy of data collection tailored to its special needs or concerns. The principal problem confronting my colleagues and myself was, at one level, elementary and perfectly obvious: What does it mean to be politically alienated? For decades Americans have been asked how they feel about the political process and politicians. Do they believe that people in public life are, by and large, honest? Do they think that political leaders care what the average citizen wants? Do they feel that public officials know their jobs?

6. A comprehensive report, prepared by William Nichols, on sampling and other technical features of the BAS sample is available, on request, from the Survey Research Center, University of California, 2538 Channing Way, Berkeley, Calif. 94720. Documentation is also available through the Inter-University Consortium for Political Research.

But for all the questions that have been asked and despite all the analysis over the years, we do not know whether alienation from politics means one thing or several, or indeed whether those who say they are alienated are in fact alienated. To learn better what lies behind an apparently cynical answer we selected for intensive study a number of respondents whom we had interviewed as part of the BAS. They were chosen in the following way. All questions in the original interview which might indicate how alienated a person is we combined into a single, summary measure; using this index, we ordered respondents according to how favorable (or unfavorable) their attitudes were, and divided the distribution of their scores into fifths. The last step was to select at random respondents within each quintile, choosing proportionately more from the two extreme groups. Our reasoning: they embody the orientations of interest to us in purest form; they are palpably alienated or allegiant.

Our objective: to break out of the cocoon of conventional questionnaires in order to learn what it means to score as alienated in a paper-and-pencil test or a standard interview. We conducted (and recorded) the "depth" interviews between February and July 1973. Interviewers were specially trained and directed to pounce on ambiguities, clichés, inconsistencies. They applied pressure. They asked a question, followed up and, sometimes, probed again, by design, in an effort to pin down how Americans feel about different aspects of American politics—to gauge the sincerity and strength of their sentiments, to expose contradictions, to illuminate nuances. After this grilling, lasting on the average an hour, we presented them with yet another questionnaire, to be completed in privacy and mailed back to us. We wound up with 143 respondents for whom we had both complete transcripts of their depth interviews (some tape recorders failed) and a completed questionnaire—or 195 after weighting to correct for the selection procedure; I shall call them the Mailback Sample. In sum, we gathered data in three different ways—by a standard interview, by an intensive interview and by a self-administered questionnaire. Each type of data has advantages and risks: the BAS is the largest and most solid; the Mailback is the most exhaustive and telling; the depth interviews are the richest and least reliable.

The Argument

Citizens have become more suspicious, more critical, more cynical about politics. So much more so, some suggest, that we face a crisis of confidence. A political system, they argue, must enjoy a deep reservoir of basic support. This reservoir assures the backing of citizens, their willingness to go along with government policies whether or not they have had the chance to approve them in advance—indeed whether or not they believe them to be a good way to deal with the problems before the country. Alienation, in this view, cripples the effectiveness, and thereby threatens the stability, of the political order.[7] A government that enjoys little trust is much like a business that has poor credit. Both have a hard time getting backing—even for ventures that would restore their good name. Shaky enterprises are hard pressed to secure support, for any venture is risky if an enterprise is shaky.

Moreover, on the grounds that citizens are disillusioned with politics, a variety of political changes have

7. For the best (and most concise) explication of this argument see James S. Coleman, "Comment on 'On the Concept of Influence,'" *Public Opinion Quarterly* 27 (Spring 1963): 63-82.

been defended or excused: the multiplication of presidential primaries; the imposition of formal restrictions on presidential powers—for example, the budgetary reform act; the diffusion of influence in Congress; the fashion of investigative journalism; the recruitment of a new generation of congressional activists; the celebration of the eclipse of machine politics; the enfeeblement of the political parties and rise of single-issue politics. The net effect, some argue, is to encourage public officials to promise more, yet leave them able to deliver less; to turn the public's loss of confidence into a vicious circle, with more and more feeling that things are getting worse— even when they happen to be getting better; in short, to raise the issue of the governability of democracies.[8]

I am not unsympathetic to this view. But it seems to me useful to reverse the customary question—to ask whether allegiance, as well as alienation, may be a problem. It can. And we shall see this once we see that there are two quite distinct types of allegiance. The difference between the two centers on a readiness to recognize that government need not be good in all respects, even if it is good in most. In terms of commonly used measures, the two are indistinguishable. But a distinction between them can and should be drawn, for one involves a judgment of government that is balanced, the other a judgment that is one-sided.

Who would expect more than a handful to think the government is good in nearly every respect and bad in none? Who would doubt that citizens holding to so extraordinary a view of government would prove, on the average at least, to be ill informed, poorly educated, po-

8. Two able expositions of the ungovernability thesis are: Anthony King, ed., *Why Is Britain Becoming Harder to Govern?* (London: B.B.C. Publications, 1976), and James Douglas, "The Overloaded Crown," *British Journal of Political Science* 6 (October 1976): 483-506.

litically apathetic? And yet the allegiant who lack balance, far from being a rarity, turn out to be rather sizable in number—even at a point in time and in a part of the country where to be politically cynical threatened to be socially fashionable. But it is not just a question of numbers. Zeal tends to be self-defeating in politics. Factors that encourage a person to be extremist in sentiment—the handicap of a poor education, for example, or an emotional conflict—tend to discourage him from being extremist in action: he is more likely to be apathetic or less likely to be effective. But those whose judgment lacks balance, who are overready to approve or to disapprove of government, are neither socially marginal nor psychologically crippled. And so they are as politically active, as consequential, as citizens whose judgment is balanced.

Attitudes toward authority, if my theory is sound, have two dimensions: one affective, the other cognitive. And this applies to the alienated just as it does to the allegiant. Citizens may harbor uncommonly unfavorable feelings about the government just as they may hold uncommonly favorable ones toward it—without a loss of perspective. We can, in short, distinguish the alienated citizen whose judgment of government is balanced from the one whose judgment is one-sided, even though both are equally cynical about politics and politicians.

We shall miss or mistake much of the significance of the wave of political cynicism which has washed over this country unless we take into account the fact that many citizens are alienated but their judgment of government is balanced. There is a civil temper, a way of thinking which is congenial to a democratic society, and a vital aspect of it is balance. We may, without intending to, confuse being civil with being well behaved or, worse, with being agreeable. But a citizen may be thoroughly alienated—he may entertain the most unflattering thoughts about the country's leadership; he may be persuaded the government is corrupt—and yet be civil.

By civil I mean certain habits of mind that favor a pluralist politics. But I also mean certain forms of conduct, the most debatable of them being protest. The role of protest in a liberal society is subject to dispute partly—though only partly—because we do not know or cannot agree on the facts of the matter; in a representative sample of the national population there are too few protestors to analyze. And that is a happy feature of this study: a sizable number who have actually engaged in a variety of forms of political protest.

In my view, certain forms of protest suit a pluralist politics: they represent an enlargement of more familiar ideas of citizen participation; they do not reflect a repudiation of conventional politics or the political order. There are, then, at least two questions to answer. First, which types of protest appear congenial and which more problematic in a democratic society? Second, to what extent is the connection between alienation and protest a function not so much of how a person feels toward the political order as of the way he thinks about it—that is, of whether his judgment is balanced or not? Democratic citizenship involves a sense of limits, and it is this sense which a balanced judgment both reflects and reinforces in behavior as well as belief.

It is the way that citizens think about political authority specifically, not the way they think generally, that I want to explore. And there is a difference. Politics aside, citizens whose judgment of government is balanced and those whose judgment is not are much alike. They sound the same when they talk of work, or their families, or the cost of housing; one is no more given than the other to oversimplification, to thinking in either-or terms, to favoring extreme views. But when it comes to politics, to a judgment of government, some citizens do lose their sense of perspective, of balance. And that is what is of interest —how citizens react when authority becomes controversial.

My view is this: Alienation of course may be a threat to the political order but as a rule it helps assure the stability and quality of a democratic politics. The issue is not whether the consequences of alienation may be good or bad, for they can be either or both; and disillusion is a normal part of the political process—however much we would rather regard it as an aberration. That is why I take the question, in the end, to be this: Under what conditions can a democratic polity tolerate, or even benefit from, political discontent and disorder?

2

Allegiance
and the
Good Citizen

Alienation, if sufficiently pervasive and profound, poses obvious dangers to a democratic political order. But obvious dangers are not the only dangers. Indeed, allegiance may pose at least as serious a threat to democratic politics as alienation, as I shall attempt to show.

The Idea of Allegiance

Thinking about how to think about allegiance is not easy. Evaluative attitudes toward authority pose a special problem that has escaped notice. Consequently, I shall proceed by a circuitous route, considering a hypothetical example much closer to home than government—attitudes toward father.

Suppose that two brothers came before us, each claiming to hold his father in higher esteem than the other, both asking us to judge who had the more favorable opinion of their father. Suppose further that an overcrowded calendar forced us to resort to a quick test of the claimants' cases. In the circumstances, we might put to both sons a number of questions, asking them, for example, whether their father was honest, reliable, good humored, forgetful, occasionally irritable and so on. For the sake of argument, let us suppose that the older son replied that his father possessed all the favorable qualities we inquired about and none of the unfavorable ones. In contrast, the younger son replied that his father had most of the favorable qualities and two or three of the unfavorable ones. Which son holds the more favorable opinion of his father?

The answer to this question seems obvious, or so social scientists studying attitudes toward authority have assumed. We proceed here as we do elsewhere, awarding bonus or penalty points depending upon whether the sentiment expressed is favorable or unfavorable. Thus, if we wished to build an index of political allegiance, we might assign a score of +1 for every response favorable to the system of government and a score of -1 for every response unfavorable to it. At the end we would add up the scores that each subject had earned. The higher the score, the more favorable the attitude.

Playing by these scoring rules, the older son wins hands down. After all, he contended that all of the favorable characteristics properly described his father while none of the unfavorable ones fitted at all. Similarly, citizens can be rank-ordered according to the number of favorable and unfavorable statements about the government they accept; the more favorable and the fewer unfavorable statements an individual endorses, the more allegiant he is.[1]

1. All studies of political alienation and allegiance have followed this algorithm. For an excellent collection of relevant articles see Ada W. Finifter, *Alienation and the Social System* (New York: Wiley, 1972). Also see Donald E. Stokes, "Popular Evaluation of Government: An Empirical Assessment," in H. Cleveland and H. D. Lasswell, eds., *Ethics and Bigness* (New York: Harper and Row, 1962), pp. 61-72; Arthur H. Miller, "Political Issues and Trust in Government," *American Political Science Review* 68 (1974): 951-972; Jack Citrin, "Comment," ibid., pp. 973-988.

Nor is my own early work an exception. See Jack Citrin, et al., "Personal and Political Sources of Alienation," *British Journal of Political Science* 5 (1975): 1-31, and Paul M. Sniderman, et al., "Stability of Support for the

But a moment's reflection should give us reason to pause before awarding a summary judgment in favor of the older son. We might never have met or heard of their father. Nevertheless, we do know that no person is perfect—including fathers. The younger son acknowledges this; the older son refuses to do so. Were we psychologists, we might toy with the idea that the older son's contention that his father is altogether perfect might well mask a considerable measure of hostility toward the father. In any event, we would not immediately declare in favor of the older son, for the younger son's evaluation of their father, precisely because it acknowledges shortcomings as well as virtues, seems on its face to be more honest, evenhanded, judicious, trustworthy—in a word, more balanced.

Two Species of Allegiance

Political systems are like parents in one respect: none is perfect. All forms of government fall short of their ideals. But public contention about this gap between principle and practice has much to do with the vitality of the democratic process itself. The viability of democratic politics depends on the ability of those out of power to challenge those in power, to bring their case before the public, to criticize policies and performance, to call for change, to compete for office. A democratic system provides both means and incentives to mount public challenges. Competitive elections encourage the "outs" to persuade voters

Political System: The Initial Impact of Watergate," *American Politics Quarterly* 3 (1975): 437-457. For a warning on this point see Geraint Parry, "Trust, Distrust, and Consensus," *British Journal of Political Science* 6 (1976): 129-142, and David Marsh, "Beliefs about Democracy among English Adolescents: What Significance Have They?" ibid., 2 (1972): 255-259.

that the "ins" have performed miserably and should therefore be put out of office. Even among the ins the pressures of political competition and individual ambition encourage one arm of government to criticize another. So congressmen criticize Congress and the administration, the administration criticizes Congress and congressmen, and the media publicize the criticisms of many against most. Both the formal and informal institutions of democratic politics legitimize, and to a degree encourage, attempts to publicize the imperfections of those who hold office and, on occasion, even of the political system itself.

What should citizens make of this? If we tread the path of precedent, we should conclude that the more good qualities he notices, the more allegiant he is. But surely this is an odd way to conceive of the notion of allegiance in a democratic system. What seems in order is not blind loyalty but balanced judgment: an awareness that a democratic political order, whatever its virtues, will have shortcomings.

Perhaps, then, we should distinguish two aspects of allegiance. Imagine two citizens, both of whom have uncommonly positive feelings toward the political system. Imagine further that we present to both a number of questions as we did to the two brothers and that these two citizens answer similarly. The citizen replying that the government possesses all or virtually all of the favorable qualities we inquired about and none of the unfavorable ones typifies one species of allegiant citizen, whom I shall call the "committed." The citizen declaring that the government possesses many favorable qualities and one or two unfavorable ones typifies a quite different species, whom I shall call "supportive."

To plunge right in, this study focuses on evaluative attitudes toward the national government, relying on an adjective checklist as a linchpin of measurement. Checklists have a spotted career: the device is well known, if variously regarded, by psychologists.[2] During the initial interview we presented our respondents with a list of adjectives, asking them to place an X beside each one they considered a good description of what they felt the national government to be like. The list contained eighteen words in all, and the percentages checking each are presented in table 1.

Respondents were free to check a particular adjective, or to pass it by unmarked. They were under no pressure to check a particular number of adjectives, let alone any given adjective (indeed, only two—"wasteful" and "confusing"—elicited a widespread response). Of the eighteen adjectives, ten were favorable, eight unfavorable.

I shall pass over the checklist without comment, apart

TABLE 1. ADJECTIVES CHECKED AS A GOOD
DESCRIPTION OF THE NATIONAL GOVERNMENT
(BAS)

Adjective	Proportion checking (N = 1,000)	Adjective	Proportion checking (N = 1,000)
Honest	25%	Trustworthy	16%
Unfair	31	Unselfish	7
Helpful	39	Wasteful	72
Corrupt	30	Stubborn	26
Kind	14	Honorable	20
Unfriendly	16	Confusing	64
Fair	36	Democratic	33
Dependable	27	Disgusting	19
Stupid	15	Efficient	14

Note: The Bay Area Survey (BAS) is the complete cross-sectional sample; for details see Chapter One.

2. See Sharon Masterson, "The Adjective Checklist Technique: A Review and Critique," in Paul McReynolds, ed., *Advances in Psychological Assessment*, vol. 3 (San Francisco: Jossey-Bass, 1975), pp. 275-312.

from two brief remarks. First, a frequent problem with this format, as administered here, is a differential willingness of individuals to check adjectives. This can become a serious problem for tests of the usual length (200 to 400 adjectives), but for a test as brief as this one there is no evidence of bias. Second, the task before the respondent is not whether to agree with a particular statement but whether to check an adjective when he is under no pressure to check any particular number of adjectives, let alone any given adjective. The fact that he is free not to respond, without suggesting that he is ignorant about the matter, or cannot bring himself to make up his mind, is critical. If we take the same adjectives (e.g., "honest") and force respondents to choose between them and their opposites, the distinction between the supportive and the committed vanishes from sight: both are equally likely to select the adjective "honest." In short, the adjective checklist as administered here is ideally suited to our purposes, not least because it minimizes pressure to respond at all.

Our aim is to identify two sets of respondents—the committed and the supportive—both of whom are highly favorable in their attitudes toward the national government. But the attitude of the committed is more than merely, or even markedly, favorable. Their view of the government appears so positive as to be exaggerated, to be less than balanced. The diagnostic sign of being committed, as I use the term here, is an uncommon willingness to praise government and an uncommon unwillingness to find fault with it. Figure 1 depicts graphically the cutting points defining the committed.

The horizontal axis in figure 1 represents the number of favorable adjectives checked. To be classified as committed an individual had to select no fewer than three favorable adjectives as good descriptions of what he or she thought the national government was like. The leni-

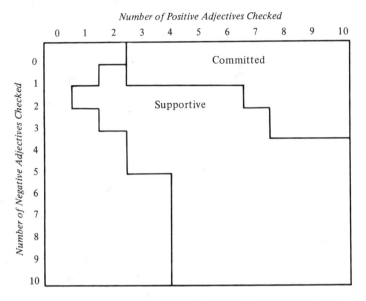

FIG. 1. AN OPERATIONAL DISTINCTION BETWEEN THE COMMITTED AND THE SUPPORTIVE.

ency of this cutting point might give the impression that the committed sprawl about. That would be quite wrong: two-thirds of them check five or more favorable adjectives. The mean number of favorable adjectives checked by all respondents other than the committed or the supportive was 0.35; in contrast, the mean number for the committed was 5.73.

The vertical axis depicts the number of unfavorable adjectives checked. In general, the more favorable adjectives an individual checked, the more unfavorable ones he or she was allowed to check. For example, if an individual checked eight favorable adjectives, thereby far exceeding the sample as a whole, it scarcely seemed unreasonable to allow him to check up to three unfavorable ones and still regard him as committed. This is partly a matter of prudence—a recognition that no measuring instrument (including most emphatically this checklist) is perfect—and partly a matter of reality (after all, nearly three-quarters of the sample checked the unfavorable adjective "wasteful" and nearly two-thirds checked "confusing," both of which are, so to speak, political clichés of the common culture). Even so, the average number of unfavorable adjectives checked by the committed was less than one, or to be precise 0.94, compared with 4.39 among all respondents except for the committed and the supportive. In sum, despite the latitude allowed by the cutting point, the committed are uncommonly willing to praise the government, and virtually unwilling to criticize it.

The supportive, as figure 1 shows, are defined as those whose feelings toward the national government on the whole are positive, but not indiscriminately so.[3] Again, the more favorable adjectives they check, the more unfavorable adjectives they may check. By a person with a supportive outlook I mean one whose orientation toward the national government is positive, but whose approval of it is not without substantial qualification or reservation. Compared with all other respondents, the supportive are somewhat favorable in their feeling toward the government (2.95 positive adjectives checked and 2.46 negative adjectives) without going overboard, as do the committed, in praise of the government. The supportive, so defined, constitute twenty-six percent of the sample as a whole, the committed twenty-three percent.

3. It is not a necessary condition, though it is a typical one, that to be classified as supportive one must check more positive than negative adjectives. There are, quite simply, no magical ratios or lines dividing the groups, in part because of the eccentricities of the stimulus words. Specifically, all negatives are not alike; two of them, "wasteful" and "confusing," are innocuous, and very popular. But the findings are the same whether they are counted or not, a point on which I have satisfied myself after building and rebuilding the typology using eight different sets of cutting points.

Some may quarrel with where I have drawn the line between the committed and the supportive. In survey analysis, cutting points are always approximate, never exact. But to say that they are approximate is not to say that they are arbitrary. The findings I shall report are not a function of selecting and relying on one and only one set. Obviously, the conceptual distinction between the committed and the supportive could be operationally drawn using a variety of cutting points. I could have insisted, for example, that the committed must check four favorable adjectives rather than three, or five rather than four. But to make sure that the findings were in no sense a product of an arbitrary (or chance) selection of cutting points, I tested no fewer than eight distinct sets, varying the number of both favorable and unfavorable adjectives that a respondent would have to have checked in order to be classified as committed. The results were always the same.

Moreover, the cutting points I settled on decreased rather than increased the magnitude of the differences observed between the committed and the supportive. Obviously, the standards for inclusion—what one had to do to be counted as committed—were far from severe. All a respondent needed to do was check three favorable adjectives and no more than one unfavorable adjective. In general, the higher or more severe the standards for selection, the purer or more ideal-typical would be the respondents selected. And the more rigorous the standards, the larger the difference observed between the committed and the supportive. But I settled on the least rigorous standards for being classified as committed, because the less rigorous the standards, the larger the number of respondents for analysis. Since many of the most telling questions were in the Mailback Survey, which was administered to only a sub-sample of the original sample, there was little alternative but to pay the price of diluting the purity of the group of most interest to me—the committed.

Aspects of Allegiance

The signs of allegiance, if not its meaning, are well established. Allegiance refers to a sense of identification with the political system and trust, confidence and pride in it. Characteristically, the allegiant citizen in a democratic society believes that its basic political institutions and values are legitimate; that government is responsive to the voices and votes of citizens (if not always immediately or perfectly so); that public leaders, though not free of human failings, are by and large decent, well intentioned and trustworthy.

Allegiance, of course, is a matter of degree. Some people are less favorable than others in their attitudes toward government and the political system, but to say that they are less favorable is not to say that they are unfavorable. It is not just citizens whose opinions are the most favorable who are allegiant, any more than it is just those in an audience who clap loudest who enjoy the show. The supportive may not be as quick to praise the political system as the committed. Nevertheless, the supportive are plainly allegiant, as we shall now see.

Consider the matter of pride. We asked respondents to choose between the following two statements:

A. I am proud of many things about our system of government.

B. I can't find much in our system of government to be proud of.

With virtual unanimity, both the committed and the supportive declare their pride in the system of government (96 and 93 percent, respectively). But as table 2 shows, there is a sharp difference in sentiment between the supportive (and the committed) and the remainder of the respondents. Only seven percent of the supportive assert that they cannot "find much in our system of government to be proud of," compared with forty percent of the rest of the sample.

TABLE 2. CONVENTIONAL INDICATORS OF ALLEGIANCE
(% DOWN – BAS)

	Committed (N = 226)	Supportive (N = 256)	All others (N = 518)
1. (a) I am proud of many things about our system of government.	96%	93%	57%
(b) I can't find much in our system of government to be proud of.	4	7	43
2. (a) The way this country is going, I often feel that I really don't belong here.	3	5	14
(b) Although our country may be facing difficult times, I still feel that it's a worthwhile place and that I really belong here.	97	95	86
3. (a) Our government officials usually tell us the truth.	84	63	26
(b) Most of the things that government leaders say can't be believed.	16	35	74
4. (a) There is almost no way people like me can have an influence on the government.	24	36	65
(b) People like me have a fair say in getting the government to do the things we care about.	76	64	35

If we look at the opposite side of the coin, at feelings of estrangement as opposed to attachment, the results are the same: ninety-seven percent of the committed and ninety-five percent of the supportive reject the proposition that "the way this country is going, I often feel I really don't belong here" in favor of the statement that "although our country may be in fairly difficult times, I still feel that it's a worthwhile place and that I really belong here." Once again the supportive are the same as the committed and the two of them are different from the rest of the sample. Fully fourteen percent of the latter are willing to take the extreme step of declaring that they don't feel that they belong in their own country, compared with only five percent of the supportive.

Admittedly, these questions are not the most sensitive tests of attachment, if only because the respondent is virtually required to disown his country to show his discontent. Consequently, it may be useful to focus on a less extreme item, one that affords the citizen an opportunity to express any dissatisfaction he may harbor without having, as it were, to disavow the political order itself. Consider, therefore, the question of whether citizens feel that they can depend on government officials to tell the truth. The difference between the supportive and the rest of the sample is impressive: sixty-three percent of the supportive declared that "our government officials usually tell us the truth," as compared with twenty-six percent of the remainder of the sample; conversely, seventy-four percent of the latter, compared with only thirty-five percent of the former, asserted that "most things that government leaders say can't be believed." To be sure, the committed are even more favorable in their views than the supportive. But to say that the committed, above all others, hold a high opinion of government officials' veracity is not to say that the supportive hold a low opinion. Just the opposite is the case, for the supportive, in overwhelming numbers, cast a vote of confidence in government officials. It is the strikingly large difference in outlook between the supportive and the rest of the sample, not the comparatively small difference between the committed and the supportive, that stands out. To cite one last example, we asked respondents to choose between the following two statements:

A. There is almost no way people like me can have an influence on government.
B. People like me can have a fair say in getting the government to do the things we care about.

The supportive and the rest of the sample, forced to choose between these two options, line up on opposite sides of the fence. Sixty-four percent of the supportive declare that people like themselves "can have a fair say in getting the government to do the things we care about." In contrast, sixty-five percent of the rest of the sample insist that there is almost no way that they or others like them can influence the government.

In sum, the supportive characteristically feel that they belong; that they can take pride in our system of government; that government officials are honest and trustworthy; that our government is open, allowing citizens a fair say. Whether we look at the matter in absolute or relative terms, the supportive are plainly allegiant. When required to choose between two statements, one favorable to the political system and the other unfavorable, the largest number of the supportive chose the former. To be sure, the supportive are not as favorable in their attitudes toward government as the committed. But this is no more than to say that our empirical findings are consistent with our operational definitions, for the committed, after all, are defined by their greater readiness to express favorable opinions about the government. What matters, certainly for the purpose at hand, is not the occasional small difference between the committed and the supportive but the invariable, striking difference between the supportive and the rest of the sample—even in regard to questions that go beyond the political clichés now in fashion and address deep-seated feelings of pride and belonging. The supportive are without question allegiant.

Contrasting Two Forms of Allegiance

Allegiance need not be blind. The supportive know that the government is not good in all respects and indeed may be bad in some. Their attachment is strong, but their judgment is balanced. In contrast, the committed embrace the political order without reservation. Theirs is a totalistic faith, and it is the politics of faith that I now wish to explore, looking at four aspects of attitudes toward authority: the importance of social control, government rights and citizen duties, civil liberties and civil rights, and political deference.

The Importance of Social Control
Commitment to a democratic system of government is not the same thing as commitment to democratic principles of governance. Indeed, the more attached a citizen is to such a system of government, the more difficult he may find it to embrace some of its cardinal principles. One reason for this apparent paradox is the central place the democratic ideal assigns to opposition to authority. Freedom of speech, for example, entails not only the freedom to speak for an idea; it entails, too, the freedom to speak against an idea. And, once garbed in the cloak of freedom of advocacy, a citizen is entitled to speak against not only ideas but men, including those in high office.

Even more, he is entitled to speak against the government itself.

A dilemma is built into the democratic idea. On the one hand, a democratic government, like any other government, depends for its success on compliance. The effectiveness and life chances of any political system hinge on the willingness of citizens to support, or at a minimum to comply with, its decisions, laws, regulations and the like. And presumably the greater the commitment of citizens to the system of government, the surer their compliance. On the other hand, the more committed citizens are to the system of government, the less willing they may be to speak against claims of authority, even when unwarranted. Trust in government, if excessive, may incline them to be overready to support government. Total faith is blind faith. Support of our system of government in this sense can place our form of government itself in jeopardy.

Consider the question of social control. The argument for social control, for the primacy of political authority over individual liberty, may rest on a view of human nature as instinctually rebellious. In this view, impulse and appetite must be kept under tight rein. Civil conduct entails social sanctions, for men lack in sufficient measure internal controls—conscience, character, superego or whatever one wishes to call them—to restrain their instincts and desires. The need for social control, on this ground, flows from a neo-Hobbesian view of man as predator, even in civil society.

The data at hand furnished several illustrations of the connection between commitment and the need for social control so conceived. In the Mailback Survey, for example, we asked what might happen if people were not closely regulated by strong laws. As table 3 shows, the committed are more likely than the supportive to reply that they would "behave like animals," while the supportive are more likely to declare that even without the yoke of strong laws most men would "behave decently." Of course, it is one thing to believe as an abstract proposition in the need for strong laws to control man's "animal" instincts. A question more directly on target is whether a person believes that tighter controls or more freedom would be better for the country, as things stand now. On this point, the reactions of the committed and the supportive differ sharply. As table 3 shows, the committed in overwhelming numbers favor more control rather than more freedom: eighty-six percent of them think that "laws that put tighter controls on behavior of people" would be best for the country as things now stand, compared with forty-nine percent of the supportive. Conversely, the supportive are nearly four times as likely as the committed to favor taking the path of de-

TABLE 3. SOCIAL CONTROL
(% DOWN – MAILBACK)

	Committed (N = 31)	Supportive (N = 66)
If people were not closely regulated by strong laws, most of them would		
Behave like animals	75%	54%
Behave decently	25	46
As things stand now, which would be best for the country?		
Laws that put tighter controls on behavior of people	86	49
Laws that give men even more freedom than they have now	14	51

The Mailback is the special sub-sample drawn from the BAS (see table 1); for details see Chapter One.

All tables omit "undecided" responses. Differences reported are significant at $p \leqslant .05$.

creased control. Thus, fifty-one percent of the supportive preferred laws that would give people "even more freedom than they have now," compared with only fourteen percent of the committed.

Government Rights and Citizen Duties

Balancing the rights of government against those of the citizen raises complex and vexing questions. Often there are rights on both sides, which have to be taken into account and weighed according to circumstances. No position is always correct. Yet, if we look at examples where the rights of government and of citizens are at odds with one another, or seem to be so, we can see a clear difference in where the broad sympathies of the committed and the supportive lie. The committed are more likely to take the side of government. Thus, sixty-nine percent think government should have the right to require citizens to serve in the armed forces during peacetime, compared with only thirty-one percent of the supportive. Even if we turn to the far more complex issue of civil disobedience, the supportive have less enthusiasm for translating the rights of government into duties of citizens. As table 4 shows, the committed are more likely than the supportive to insist that government should have the right to make someone obey a law that goes against his conscience.

The point, let me emphasize, is not that the supportive are always more inclined than the committed to side with the citizen rather than the government. Indeed, over a broad range of issues they are just as willing to uphold the rights of government. Thus, they are just as likely as the committed to agree that government should have the right to require citizens to serve the country in some way during a war they disapprove of, or to require citizens to help a policeman if he asks them for assistance (data not shown). Rather, the point is that the supportive show a

TABLE 4. GOVERNMENT RIGHTS AND CITIZEN DUTIES
(% DOWN – MAILBACK)

	Committed (N = 31)	Supportive (N = 66)
Should government have the right to make someone obey a law that goes against his conscience?		
Yes	83%	60%
No	17	40
Should government have the right to require citizens to serve in the armed forces during peacetime?		
Yes	69	31
No	31	69

reflectiveness that the committed do not. The supportive sometimes side with the government, sometimes not, depending on the specific question at issue. The committed —or at any rate, a majority of them—side with the government. On nearly every question we asked about government rights and citizens' duties, the committed cast their lot with the government, and overwhelmingly so. They approve of the government without reservation; they side with it virtually without exception.

Civil Liberties

A willingness to side with government takes on a special importance in the area of civil liberties and civil rights. We should expect the committed to favor the primacy of political authority over the principles of individual liberty to the extent that they see the issue as one entailing a need either to establish control over men's "animal appetites" or to give a vote of confidence to the government (or an agency of government such as the police).

Consider freedom of the press. We asked our respondents whether "closing down magazines that print dirty pictures would improve the country's morals" or "violate people's rights." The committed are twice as likely as the supportive to favor banning pornography. As we see in table 5, forty-four percent of the committed believe that forbidding publication of magazines "that print dirty pictures would improve the country's morals," compared with twenty-one percent of the supportive; the latter are more likely than the former to believe that such a step would "violate people's rights." Or consider the issue of tapping telephones. This is an issue where right and wrong are less clear, even to civil libertarians. There are surely some circumstances where tapping may be proper. The committed and the supportive differ on this question, but the difference is understandably smaller than on the question of banning pornography. Half of the committed declare that "tapping telephones of people suspected of planning crimes is essential to good police work"; in contrast, sixty-five percent of the supportive believe that such action "should be prohibited as an invasion of privacy."

TABLE 5. CIVIL LIBERTIES
(% DOWN – MAILBACK)

	Committed (N = 31)	Supportive (N = 66)
Closing down magazines that print dirty pictures would		
Improve the country's morals	44%	21%
Violate people's rights	56	79
Tapping telephones of people suspected of planning crimes		
Is essential to good police work	50	35
Should be prohibited as an invasion of privacy	50	65

It would be an oversimplification to conclude that the supportive are civil libertarians and the committed are not. If the matter were indeed that simple, the question I have put, distinguishing between these two groups according to whether their orientation toward government is balanced or not, would be a good deal less interesting than, in fact, it is.

To begin with, we should note that at least half of the committed take the side of individual liberties on both of these questions. Admittedly, they are not as likely as the supportive to rally around, say, freedom of the press in this instance. But this is not to say that the bulk of them are anti-civil libertarian. More importantly, if we consider other questions that deal with different aspects of these two problems—a free press and the rights of those accused of crime—we see that it would be wrong to suggest that the committed are anti-civil libertarian, even in comparison with the supportive. For example, by virtually identical majorities, both the committed and the supportive insist that "forbidding the sale of books that promote the revolutionary overthrow of government would violate constitutional rights," rather than be "a sensible way to defend the Constitution." Moreover, both declare, by a similar margin, that "in dealing with the crime problem, the most important consideration is to protect the rights of the accused," and not to "stop crime even if we have to violate the rights of the accused." The committed, then, favor tapping telephones and banning pornography most likely because of the importance they attach to establishing control and siding with authority, not because of a hostility to civil liberties and civil rights per se.

Deference to Government
The committed, I have argued, are overready to side with authority because they are overready to approve of

authority. If I am right in this, the committed should display a distinctly defensive attitude toward the political order—a willingness to "go along" with it even when it may have done wrong, an unwillingness to criticize it even if it has done wrong. We asked respondents to choose between the following two statements.

A. I think Americans should be willing to defend what their country does, even if they feel it has done something wrong.
B. If our country does something wrong, we should be prepared to criticize it.

As table 6 shows, two-thirds of the committed take the position of "my country, right or wrong." In contrast, nearly sixty percent of the supportive take the opposite view, insisting on the legitimacy of criticism. It is not a matter of disliking or disapproving of criticism in, say, a crisis. Rather, the committed's position quite simply is that it is wrong to criticize one's country even when it has

TABLE 6. DEFERENCE TO GOVERNMENT
(% DOWN − MAILBACK)

	Committed (N = 31)	Supportive (N = 66)
I think Americans should be willing to defend what their country does, even if they feel it has done something wrong.	66%	43%
or		
If our country does something wrong, we should be prepared to criticize it.	34	57
There are times when it is necessary for the government to bend or even break the law if it is to do its job.		
Agree	58	25
Disagree	42	75

done something wrong. Criticizing the idea of criticism under these conditions is tantamount to rejecting the propriety of criticism altogether.

Such an attitude can have dangerous consequences. Consider what choice the committed make when they find themselves under pressure to uphold a patently unwarranted claim by government. One section of the Mailback Survey opened with the following introductory statement:

Here are some things most Americans agree with, but we would like to know your opinion about them anyway. If you agree with a statement, please put a check in the "agree" box; if you disagree with it, put a check in the "disagree" box.

We then asked, among other things, whether "there are times when it's necessary for the government to bend or even break the law if it is to do its job." Comparing the committed and the supportive on this point, we see that the difference between them is impressive: six out of every ten of the committed are willing to give the government the right to do whatever it pleases in order "to do its job," even if it means violating the law; in contrast, only one in four of the supportive are so inclined. Surely, there is no need to waste ink underlining the significance of such a proposition's being able to command public support. To the extent that citizens tolerate or, worse, encourage violation of the law by government, we have no government of law.

In sum, the committed distinguish themselves by their enthusiasm for control—in insisting on the need for strong laws if men are to behave decently rather than like animals, and in favoring, as things now stand, tighter controls rather than more freedom. Then, too, their high opinion of government and their low opinion of their fellow citizens inclines them at times to show less enthusiasm than the supportive for freedom of the press and the right to privacy. Last, the committed distinguish themselves by their deference to authority—by their rejection of the propriety of criticism of the country and their overreadiness to countenance government's bending or breaking the law—not to protect national security, or to preserve world peace, or to avoid a nuclear holocaust, but merely "to do its job."

The Question of the Good Citizen

The supportive come closer to being good citizens in a democratic society than the committed. But in showing that the supportive are better citizens I do not mean to suggest that they are the best citizens. To be sure, they are more likely than the committed to resist unwarranted claims of the state. But the evidence I have presented should not be taken to mean that they will on all occasions resist such claims.

Moreover, it is one thing to object in a public opinion survey to attempts by government to break the law; it is quite another thing to express one's objection publicly—to one's friends and family, let alone to newspapers, public officials or politically prominent figures. More broadly, it is one thing to believe that the government is attempting to break the law, and quite another to do something about it. Whether and when citizens, persuaded that the government is attempting to break the law, would act on their beliefs is a question which calls for an answer.

Furthermore, I have rested my case on a limited, and in some respects an atypical, range of circumstances. As we have seen, the supportive are far less willing than the committed to condone attempts by the government to bend or break the law. This outcome may be comforting to those who care about the democratic idea. But there are surely no grounds for being sanguine. How many citizens who are willing to oppose attempts by government to bend or break the law are likely, in a specific situation, to recognize that what the government is attempting to do is just that? In asking the question as we did—and had to do—we also gave part of the answer, namely, that what the government wanted to do was illegal. Worse, we made it plain that it wanted to get around the law for no better reason than "to do its job"—as opposed, say, to having to fend off a clear threat to world peace.

Plainly, the questions at issue are complex; they are unlikely to yield to any simple, authoritative answers. The reactions of the supportive to the claims of the state concerning citizens' obligations and duties depend to an important degree on the specific issues at stake and the exact language in which they are couched. Precisely when and where the supportive are prepared to draw a line, and reject the claim of the state to compliance, is a question to which I have offered only the beginning of an answer.

Whatever the answer may turn out to be, the supportive have shown themselves to be better citizens than the committed, presumably because the orientation of the supportive toward government is balanced, while that of the committed is not. But there is much about this notion of a balanced orientation, and the uses I put it to, which may be unclear. Although I shall not comment at length now, at least one or two remarks are in order. Whether one's judgment is balanced is a matter of degree. To speak otherwise, as I have done, is to acknowledge how crude the procedures of measurement in fact are. But so that there may be no misunderstanding on this point, I wish to emphasize how serious a mistake it would be to treat the distinction between the committed and the supportive as hard and fast, as though it were set in cement.

Even apart from genuine problems of measurement, the danger of misunderstanding remains. Though I cannot prove it, I incline to the view that the distinction between the supportive and the committed—and more particularly the scores on the adjective checklist on which this distinction is based—is a product of the play between the psychological makeup of individuals and the political circumstances of the moment. On the one side, I have some doubt whether the committed would rally around the government as they do, insisting that it possesses virtually every favorable quality conceivable, if the spirit of the times were not so critical and antagonistic and if the incumbent president had not been a conservative Republican under attack. On the other side, I suspect that many of the supportive would have attributed a number of favorable adjectives to the government (e.g., "honest") were it not for the prevailing climate of opinion and the bitter experiences that lie behind it. In short, the distinction between the committed and the supportive may chiefly be of value in time of political discontent and disillusion.

Moreover, what constitutes a lack of balance is an open question. Is it the overreadiness to believe that the government possesses desirable qualities? Or is it the unwillingness to acknowledge that it possesses virtually any undesirable quality? Or is it both? I have no conclusive answer to this question. And indeed our perplexity is likely to grow.

The Politics of Unreason

The politics of unreason wears many faces, among them prejudice, superpatriotism, authoritarianism, chauvinism, isolationism, ignorance of or outright opposition to basic civil liberties and civic rights, extremist ideologies and electoral support of extremist candidates. Thanks to systematic studies by social scientists we have become familiar with the psychology and sociology of many of these faces.[4] Sentiments that are illiberal and antidemocratic in spirit chiefly find their home in American society among those who find it harder to learn, whether because of their social circumstances or psychological makeup, the fundamental values of the official culture.

Commitment, too, is an expression of the politics of unreason. But it is in a decisive respect different from familiar forms of right-wing extremism. Chauvinism appeals most to the unenlightened and inarticulate, to the poorly educated and poorly off, to those who are socially or culturally marginal.[5] Commitment, however, represents a quite different phenomenon.

To begin with, as table 7 shows, the committed are not poorly off. Twenty-seven percent of the committed earned annual incomes in excess of $15,000 in 1972, compared with thirty-four percent of the supportive. To be sure, the committed are less well educated than the supportive; but measured against any reasonable standard they are not poorly educated: thirty-four percent of them have entered or finished college.[6] Nor are the committed the uprooted.

4. For example, Gertrude Selznick and Stephen Steinberg, *The Tenacity of Prejudice* (New York: Harper and Row, 1969); Herbert McClosky, "Personality and Attitude Correlates of Foreign Policy Orientation," in James Rosenau, ed., *Domestic Sources of Foreign Policy* (New York: The Free Press, 1967), pp. 51-110; Herbert McClosky and John H. Schaar, "Psychological Dimensions of Anomy," *American Sociological Review* 30 (1965): 14-40; Seymour Martin Lipset and Earl Raab, *The Politics of Unreason: Right-Wing Extremism in America, 1790-1970* (New York: Harper and Row, 1970); Paul M. Sniderman, *Personality and Democratic Politics* (Berkeley: University of California Press, 1975).

5. These findings are a first approximation, responsive to the question here, but incomplete. See chap. 4 for results with age controlled.

6. McClosky, "Personality and Attitude Correlates." The dependent variable is isolationism, but the general argument—and the basic findings—hold for chauvinism.

TABLE 7. A DEMOGRAPHIC PROFILE OF THE COMMITTED
AND THE SUPPORTIVE
(% DOWN – BAS)

	Committed (N = 226)	Supportive (N = 256)
Income:		
Up to $4,999	15%	14%
$5,000-9,999	33	23
$10,000-14,999	26	28
$15,000 or more	27	34
Education:		
Grade school or less	16	6
Some high school	14	9
High school graduate	36	32
Some college	16	28
College graduate*	18	27
Self-designated social class:		
Working	29	25
Lower	2	1
Middle	49	56
Upper middle	20	18
Length of residence in the Bay Area:		
Less than a year	3	7
1-2 years	6	5
3-5 years	7	9
6-10 years	13	11
11-20 years	18	25
More than 20 years	54	45

*B.A. or postgraduate degree.

Fifty-four percent of the committed (compared with forty-
five percent of the supportive) have lived in the Bay Area
for twenty years or more. Then, too, the committed take
an active part in the life of the community. They are as
likely as the supportive to belong to church-connected
groups, fraternal lodges or veterans' organizations, business or civic groups, community center and neighborhood
improvement associations, social or card-playing groups,

sports teams, country clubs and charity or welfare organizations. In sum, the committed are reasonably well-to-do and well educated, and are socially integrated. In contrast, the chauvinistic tend to be poorly off, poorly educated and socially marginal. Commitment is not just chauvinism by another name.

Moreover, many of the expressions of the politics of unreason with which social scientists are most familiar, such as authoritarianism or chauvinism, appeal especially to those who are troubled by feelings of personal unworthiness or inferiority, who are given to pessimism and chronic anxiety, who display a pattern of diffuse neuroticism of which low self-esteem is a central element. But the committed are just as likely as the supportive to take a positive attitude toward themselves, to express satisfaction with themselves, to feel they can do things as well as most people. Or, to look at the opposite side of the coin, the committed are no more likely than the supportive to wish they could have more respect for themselves, to feel they are failures or to think they are no good at all. Moreover, when asked about their lives, the committed are at least as likely as the supportive to describe their lives as successful, free, interesting, secure and worthwhile. Conversely, they are as unlikely as the supportive (if not more so) to describe their lives as tense, disappointing, lonely or discouraging (data not shown).

Admittedly, the information at hand is limited. It was not part of our purpose to administer a comprehensive battery of psychological tests. Nevertheless, on the basis of voluminous research, we know that the measure of self-esteem we employed also taps a chronic sense of anxiety, authoritarianism, misanthropy, feelings of helplessness, hopelessness and loneliness, and the like.[7] This

7. Morris Rosenberg, *Convincing the Self* (New York: Basic Books, 1979); Morris Rosenberg, *Society and the Adolescent Self-Image* (Princeton: Princeton University Press, 1965); Sniderman, *Personality and Democratic Politics.*

measure of self-esteem, therefore, is an economical, albeit simple, indicator of psychological adjustment. At a minimum, there is no evidence that gross psychological maladjustment underlies commitment. In sum, the committed are not psychological cripples. The committed and the supportive may well differ in their psychological makeup, especially in their cognitive style. But commitment is not just another example of a political pathology springing from psychological pathology; commitment is not authoritarianism by another name.

Moreover, it would be one thing if this tendency to rally around the government grew out of a narrowness of mind and intolerance of spirit owing to a lack of education; or if the committed were trapped in the outer pockets of society and so at a distance from the mainstream of politics; or if they were victims of deep-seated psychological conflicts which, more often than not, are self-debilitating. If any or all of these things were true, the committed would tend to play a less active role in politics than the average citizen: they would know less, care less, do less. But none of these things is true (table 8). The committed are as interested and involved in politics as other citizens. They are as likely to follow news of national events, to watch news broadcasts on television, to read news stories in the newspapers, to be interested in American politics and government.

Commonly, citizens with little regard for core democratic values, such as procedural rights or tolerance, are socially and psychologically marginal. Many of the factors that lead them to oppose democratic values—a lack of formal schooling, low self-esteem and the like—tend also to disarm them as opponents of democratic politics. They tend to lack the personal poise and political sophistication to translate their attitudes into action. But the committed suffer no special disabilities, social or

TABLE 8. POLITICAL INTEREST AND INVOLVEMENT: A
COMPARISON OF THE COMMITTED AND THE SUPPORTIVE
(% DOWN — BAS)

Political attentiveness	Committed (N = 226)	Supportive (N = 256)
How closely do you follow the news of national events?		
Very closely	25%	27%
Pretty closely	52	47
Not too closely	23	26
How often in this last week did you watch the news broadcasts on television?		
Not at all or has no TV	14	12
Once or twice	12	17
Three or four hours	13	16
Almost every day	17	13
Every day	45	42
How often this last week did you read news stories?		
Not at all or does not read	15	14
Once or twice	12	11
Three or four times	9	13
Almost every day	11	7
Every day	54	55
How interested are you in (American) politics and government?		
Very interested	26	26
Fairly interested	44	42
Only a little interested	23	26
Not at all interested	8	7

psychological. So they can, and do, take as active a part as other citizens in the political process. They embody, therefore, an especially threatening species of the politics of unreason.

The threat they pose may not be direct, but it is no less

a threat. The politically embittered may set off a bomb, organize a street disturbance, trigger a courthouse shooting. By contrast, the committed are unlikely to hit the streets in protest. But they do constitute a public constituency, impressive in size (even in the Bay Area), politically aware and active, overanxious to rally around the government, which after all enjoys, if not a monopoly, in many directions a superfluity of power. No government, however well designed or well intentioned, will fail to make mistakes. No government enjoys immunity against unprincipled, dishonest, demagogic leaders. And the committed are overready to back those who govern, because those who govern are the government.

The Civil Temper

To appreciate the significance of the distinction that I have drawn between two species of allegiance, it is worth pausing to reflect on the habit of mind embodied in the design of the American political order. The Articles of Confederation won endorsement in 1778; after less than eight years, a hundred or so men met in Philadelphia's Independence Hall to set aside that contract and put in its stead a new constitution. Of late we seem to have lost sight of the conception of politics and the political order that governed the constitutional debate at that time—a conception which, to my mind, is a principal guardian of the democratic idea itself. The men convened in Philadelphia, having tried the Articles of Confederation, acting out of the conviction that they could learn from the failure of their initial attempt, set out to devise a new and superior political order. They undertook, as Austin Ranney has remarked, the grandest political experiment.[8]

8. Austin Ranney, "The Divine Science: Political Engineering in American Culture," *American Political Science Review* 70 (1976): 140-148.

They understood their undertaking to be an experiment, an attempt guided so far as possible by reason and experience, but a venture that must not only be unsure of success but in some important respects certain of failure—if reason and experience were any guide at all. Their principal concern was to design an institutional order to remedy, so far as possible, the political ills known to them. Coupled with this concern, however, was an awareness that new ills would surely emerge, whose exact form no person could forecast. This was not the least important reason for their introduction of a new political form: a fundamental contract stipulating that the contract itself could be amended. The remarks of Madison in the thirty-seventh *Federalist* typify this frankly experimental approach to the construction of an enduring political order.

It has been shewn in the course of these papers, that the existing Confederation is founded on principles which are fallacious; that we must consequently change this first foundation, and with it, the superstructure resting upon it. It has been shewn, that the other confederacies which could be consulted as precedents, have been viciated by the same erroneous principles, and can therefore furnish no other light than that of beacons, which give warning of the course to be shunned, without pointing out that which ought to be pursued. The most that the Convention could do in such a situation, was to avoid the errors suggested by the past experience of other countries, as well as of our own; and to provide a convenient mode of rectifying their own errors, as future experience may unfold them.[9]

It is this habit of mind, affirmative of democratic principles yet decently skeptical of human character and an uncertain future, to which I wish to call attention. By a supportive citizen I have in mind one who is committed

9. *The Federalist*, ed. Jacob E. Cooke (Middletown, Conn.: Wesleyan University Press, 1961; also paperbound, Cleveland: Meridian Books, 1961), p. 233.

to democratic principles yet is aware of the inevitable infirmities of democratic institutions, however well conceived, and of those who hold public office, however well intentioned. At a minimum, the supportive citizen recognizes that our system of government, for all its admirable qualities, does suffer shortcomings. Indeed, he may even appreciate that its vices are sometimes a byproduct of its virtues. A government that is genuinely democratic, one that truly attempts to take account of the bewildering variety and often conflicting desires of its citizens (some of which are expressed vociferously while others are muted and can be made out only with great difficulty, if at all), is likely to seem confusing and inefficient. Indeed, it is likely to be confusing and inefficient. The accommodation of a bewildering number of groups struggling for an audience and an advantage in an extraordinarily complex set of political institutions can be a staggering process.

In the end, the prospect for democratic politics depends, I believe, on an appreciation that government is not, and never can be, perfect. One must be prepared to acknowledge its imperfections, without leaping from the fact that it is imperfect to the conclusion that it is unjust. This is the danger most often spoken of nowadays. But there is another, equally serious danger. Those who refuse to acknowledge the inevitable imperfections of government, whose allegiance is without qualification or reservation, may pose as serious a threat as the most embittered to a democratic political order.

Allegiance in an authoritarian state is a fairly straightforward affair: to be allegiant is to be loyal to the government, to comply with its edicts, to support it without question or qualification. To be allegiant in a democratic society, however, is not quite so simple a matter. The allegiant citizen must both guard and guard against the state; appreciate the rights of government and the liberties of citizens; abide by laws that he dislikes or even opposes and yet insist on the rights of others to criticize laws and codes of conduct to which he may be deeply committed. There are many observers of public affairs who see in the decline of public trust in government over the last decade a reason for alarm. They speak of a crisis in confidence, a twilight of authority, a crisis in democracy. I appreciate and, to a degree, share their concern. But it strikes me as more than just barely possible that what we are witnessing at present may be not a dying of faith but a rebirth of vigilance—a prospect that should hearten rather than discourage those who care for the democratic idea.

3
Disaffection and Protest

A democratic society runs on trust. Perhaps one cannot be exact about this, but a loss of public confidence in political institutions becomes a matter of concern to the degree that the alienated have withdrawn their consent, or have hedged it about. Governing a democratic society may never be an easy business, but it is likely to be a much chancier affair when consent is conditional. Yet a democratic society also depends on opposition. It need not tolerate all forms of challenge, but it surely must put up with disapproval of the government. The question, then, is not whether citizens may disapprove but what form their disapproval may take. And in attempting an answer to this question, I believe that the quality of their judgment—above all, whether it is balanced or not—needs to be taken into account.

As we distinguished two types of allegiance so we may distinguish two types of alienation. Let us call "disaffected" those whose view of government is one-sided. Let us call "disenchanted" those whose view of government is more evenhanded. Both are alienated; yet the judgment of the second is balanced, the first is not. And this distinction between the two makes a difference. To underline what is at stake I shall focus on political protest, in particular on two of its principal forms and their connection to alienation.

Types of Alienation

What more exactly do I mean by disaffected, and by disenchanted? Just as I used the adjective checklist to distinguish between the committed and the supportive, so I shall rely on it to distinguish the disaffected and the disenchanted. Specifically, I call a person disaffected who checks at least five of the eight unfavorable adjectives.[1] I call a person disenchanted who checks no less than three and no more than four of the unfavorable adjectives, while checking no more than two of the favorable adjectives. On the basis of these cutting points, the mean number of unfavorable adjectives checked by the disaffected and the disenchanted are 6.2 and 3.5, respectively; the mean number of favorable adjectives checked are 0.3 and 0.4. So defined, the disaffected and the disenchanted comprise seventeen percent and nineteen percent of the Bay Area sample.

The disaffected and the disenchanted are both alienated; compared with anyone else, they are plainly cynical about politics. To obtain a glimpse of the strength and scope of their sentiments, we shall look at their feelings about government.

An Initial Overview

In the Mailback questionnaire we presented respondents with pairs of contrasting words or phrases that people use to describe American government and poli-

1. As in distinguishing the supportive and the committed, I used a number of cutting points, jointly varying the number of favorable and unfavorable adjectives checked, to test operational definitions of the disaffected and the disenchanted. Again the point I should like to underline is this: the findings reported are not a function of choosing some idiosyncratic and peculiarly advantageous set of cutting points. On the contrary, the results are on all points similar, on all key ones identical, over as broad a range of alternative cutting points as is consistent with the conceptual definitions.

tics. We made use of a semantic differential format, anchoring each scale with a word or phrase at one end (e.g., "represents the powerful few"), and its opposite at the other end (e.g., "represents the majority"). We employed the standard five-point scale, although we took the precaution of adding an additional response option, prominently labeled "Undecided." Last, we specifically instructed respondents to tell us how they felt about the American national government, *regardless of which party is in power.*[2]

Both the disenchanted and disaffected let loose a salvo against the government. As table 9 shows, both are far more likely than the allegiant—be they supportive or committed—to declare that the national government is corrupt, representative of the powerful few rather than the majority, unaware of important problems. Both are more likely to picture the government as shortsighted, closed-minded, immoral. Moreover, what they are reluctant to say is perhaps as important as what they do say; they find it hard to declare, without qualification, that the government deserves their loyalty, their support or even their obedience.

It would be captious to dismiss some of these sentiments as clichés, to regard them as no more than empty rituals of everyday speech. We have grown accustomed, perhaps, to bombast. Yet it is one thing for citizens to declare that they cannot trust the government to do the right thing. It is quite another for citizens to feel uncomfortable making an unqualified declaration of loyalty.

The disenchanted are less vehement than the disaffected. For example, the disaffected are more likely to contend that the national government is immoral, unfair to some races, does more harm than good, while being

2. This warning was italicized in the Mailback questionnaire.

TABLE 9. EVALUATIONS OF AMERICAN GOVERNMENT
(% DOWN – MAILBACK)

American national government:		Disaffected (N = 31)	Disenchanted (N = 41)	Middle (N = 26)	Supportive (N = 66)	Committed (N = 31)
Is corrupt	1	33%	19%	10%	0%	7%
	2	33	42	14	22	7
	3	26	22	29	48	11
	4	7	17	38	22	37
Is not corrupt	5	0	0	10	9	37
Represents the powerful few	1	54	37	26	11	11
	2	21	29	13	16	22
	3	14	18	26	35	11
Represents the	4	4	11	22	27	11
majority	5	7	5	13	11	44
Ignores important problems	1	37	8	8	5	0
	2	22	15	8	7	11
	3	19	49	28	24	11
Pays attention to	4	11	25	32	39	26
important problems	5	11	5	24	26	52

Plans for the future	1	27	8	26	34	59
	2	15	28	26	29	24
	3	39	33	26	23	14
Cares only about today	4	15	33	22	9	3
	5	4	0	0	5	0
Listens to new ideas	1	8	5	24	5	48
	2	13	16	40	56	26
	3	33	57	32	33	22
Doesn't listen to new ideas	4	25	19	0	5	4
	5	21	3	4	2	0
Is moral	1	7	5	19	3	36
	2	4	11	19	34	50
	3	30	57	38	46	11
	4	33	22	10	15	4
Is im:moral	5	26	5	14	2	0
Deserves loyalty	1	28	13	67	70	73
	2	20	40	29	20	17
	3	28	40	5	8	3
Doesn't deserve loyalty	4	4	8	0	2	7
	5	20	0	0	2	0

Table 9 (continued)

American national government:		Disaffected (N = 31)	Disenchanted (N = 41)	Middle (N = 26)	Supportive (N = 66)	Committed (N = 31)
Deserves the support of citizens	1	22	14	72	67	76
	2	7	33	12	23	14
	3	37	44	16	9	10
Does not deserve support of citizens	4	22	6	0	0	0
	5	11	3	0	2	0
Deserves to have its laws obeyed	1	37	27	70	64	80
	2	15	43	17	21	13
	3	19	24	13	14	7
Does not deserve to have its laws obeyed	4	19	5	0	0	0
	5	11	0	0	2	0
Is unfair to some races	1	45	12	16	8	4
	2	35	44	16	23	7
	3	10	20	28	42	30
Gives fair and equal treatment to all races	4	3	17	20	23	26
	5	7	7	20	5	33
Does more harm than good	1	8	0	6	2	7
	2	8	8	0	3	0
	3	54	47	17	39	11
Does more good than harm	4	19	34	28	35	26
	5	12	11	50	22	56

less likely to believe that the government really cares about individual freedom or people's needs. In short, whenever the disaffected and the disenchanted differ in their views of government, the former prove the more alienated. And yet the occasional difference between the two pales in comparison with the gulf between their outlook on the one side, and that of the supportive and the committed on the other. As the latter are plainly allegiant, the former are manifestly alienated.

In the Bay Area Survey we asked respondents how often they feel the government can be trusted to do what is right. Only ten percent of the disaffected, and seventeen percent of the disenchanted, feel that they can trust the government to do what is right just about all the time, or even most of the time. On this point the contrast between their bleak view and the optimism of the allegiant very nearly approaches that between night and day: fully fifty-five percent of the supportive, and eighty-two percent of the committed, declare that they could trust government to do what is right most or even all of the time.

If we adopt the question of credibility as our measure, the disenchanted prove themselves as fully alienated as the disaffected. For example, we asked respondents to choose one of two statements, whichever came closer to how they felt about the matter:

A. Our government officials usually tell us the truth.
B. Most of what our government leaders say can't be believed.

As table 10 shows, far and away most of the disaffected and the disenchanted insist that, as a rule, what government leaders say cannot be believed. By contrast, equally lopsided majorities among the supportive and the committed contend that government officials can be trusted to tell the truth.

Of course, the question of government credibility, at

Really cares about						
individual freedom	1	17	13	20	28	62
	2	7	0	40	40	28
	3	21	78	28	23	10
Doesn't care about	4	24	10	8	5	0
individual freedom	5	31	0	4	5	0
Really cares about	1	4	3	24	16	52
people's needs	2	7	15	44	38	30
	3	22	39	12	33	15
Only pretends to care	4	37	36	8	13	4
about people's needs	5	30	8	12	2	0
How much of the time do you think you can trust the government to do what is right?*						
— Just about all of the time		0	1	6	7	17
— Most of the time		10	16	33	48	65
— Only some of the time		72	77	54	44	17
— None of the time		18	7	7		

*RAS

least in its most overt form, is the subject of social fads and fashions. The "credibility" of government periodically disappears, and without ever having returned disappears again, if ordinary conversation is a guide. And, in part because the issue of credibility has attracted so much attention in the popular press in recent years, a climate of opinion which established a stance of disbelief as not merely legitimate but even fashionable has settled over broad circles of the society. It is especially important, therefore, to look for expressions of disbelief which are less ritualistic and more arresting.

The disenchanted and the disaffected are united in a presumption of disbelief. It is not merely a matter of their saying they won't take a government official at his word. They are cynical: people in politics don't make mistakes, they tell lies. The alienated do not lack certitude—for example, they would have us believe that people choose to be either honest or dishonest. Expediency is all, in their view: "Our political leaders are prepared to lie to us whenever it suits their purposes." Personal advantage, not the benefit of the country, dictates what political leaders say or do. A commanding majority of the disenchanted and the disaffected contend that "the main reason presidents keep information secret is so they can hide things the public would object to"; in contrast, the supportive and the committed overwhelmingly feel that "when presidents keep facts from the public, it's usually because they want to protect the national security." The cynicism of the alienated is expansive: it embraces why political leaders say what they do or fail to say anything at all.

Yet perhaps the answers we hear—the thoroughgoing and insistent cynicism of the disaffected and the disenchanted alike—spring from the questions we ask, or, more precisely, from the way we frame them. A question about

TABLE 10. INDICATORS OF CYNICISM
(% DOWN – MAILBACK)

	Disaffected (N = 31)	Disenchanted (N = 41)	Middle (N = 26)	Supportive (N = 66)	Committed (N = 31)
1. (a) Our government officials usually tell us the truth.	12%	26%	47%	65%	84%
(b) Most of what our government leaders say can't be believed.	88	74	54	35	16
2. (a) Most of our political leaders can be trusted.	8	47	52	72	86
(b) Our political leaders are prepared to lie to us whenever it suits their purposes.	92	53	48	28	14
3. (a) When presidents keep facts from the public it's usually because they want to protect the national security.	8	23	62	80	93
(b) The main reason presidents keep information secret is so they can hide things the public would object to.	92	77	38	20	7

4. (a) I'm more likely to trust what a government spokesman says than what the newspapers or television tell us.	8	13	24	50	71
(b) Newspapers and television are more likely to tell us the truth about public affairs than the people who speak for the government.	92	87	76	50	29
5. (a) Corruption is a serious problem in our government — too many of our officials are simply not honest.	84	69	38	31	15
(b) Given the pressures they face, most of our political leaders are surprisingly honest.	16	31	62	69	85
6. (a) These days almost every citizen has to be careful about what he says, because the government may be listening in.	79	61	17	28	13
(b) All the talk these days about the government spying on people is not really true.	21	39	83	72	88

the honesty of government no more admits of an absolute answer than one about the generosity of a person. When we form an impression of a person's virtues—when we say he is thoughtful, for example, we generally mean that he is more thoughtful than others. So, too, with the question of honesty in government. What we need to know is the comparative, not the absolute, level of honesty which citizens attribute to government. Thus our respondents were asked to choose between the following two statements:

- A. I'm more likely to trust what a government spokesman says than what the newspapers and television tell us.
- B. Newspapers and television are more likely to tell us the truth about public affairs than the people who speak for the government.

Faced with this choice, the disenchanted and the disaffected with near unanimity place their faith in the media; by comparison, the committed and the supportive are far more likely to put their trust in the government.

The judgment of the alienated, I believe, is not only absolute in character, but absolutist in spirit. They impress me as indifferent or unsympathetic to the reasons why in politics good men will make bad mistakes. They show a certain intolerance in their refusal to take into account, in arriving at some judgment of a political figure or event, either mitigating circumstances or human frailty itself.

We should be on the lookout, then, for an awareness of the inevitability of some human lapse, for an appreciation of the certainty that all will eventually do the wrong thing, sometimes for the right reason. An informed judgment of honesty—or, for that matter, any virtue—calls for tolerance of human frailty. And it is the judgment of the allegiant that reflects such tolerance. At a time when

charges of criminal corruption against prominent political figures had prepared the ground for reactions to
Watergate, the committed and the supportive were two
or more times as likely as the disaffected and the disenchanted to declare that "given the pressures they face,
most of our political leaders are surprisingly honest." For
the disaffected and the disenchanted, the answer was obvious and just the opposite. Politicians are venal; things
are that simple. In sum, what matters is not just the
judgment of politics that the alienated render—disenchanted as well as disaffected—but the spirit of that judgment. And that spirit is indifferent or unsympathetic to
the pressures of politics or the imperfections of men.
This shows itself in a certain exaggeration of alarm.
Consider the issue of government surveillance. Plainly,
government agencies have resorted to break-ins and other
illegal acts of surveillance, and they have done so more
often than once was commonly supposed. But to say this
is not to say that America is a police state, a society in
which every citizen must guard his tongue lest an in-
cautious word land him in jail. Yet the alienated—the
disaffected and the disenchanted alike—affect such a
suspicious manner that they declare such a state of affairs
not just a possibility but an actuality. Thus the disaffected and the disenchanted are overwhelmingly of the
view that "these days almost every citizen has to be careful about what he says, because the government may be
listening in."

Structure of Cynicism
Their cynicism is so inclusive as to be formless. It involves a disbelief in competence as well as motive, which
finds expression, for example, in the view that "most
people in government don't know enough to do their jobs
well." Disbelief attaches to all, or nearly all, political

institutions. We see in our data now-familiar signs of the
sorry state of political parties. As table 11 shows, the
disenchanted as well as the disaffected sourly observe
that the two major parties, like Tweedledee and Tweedle-
dum, "are so much alike that voters do not really get
much choice when they vote." Moreover, both tend to
dismiss the parties as "only interested in people's votes
but not in their opinions."

An anti-party spirit has long been a staple of American
politics. And elections fare little better.[3] Elections, as
practiced at present, evoke long-standing complaints;
which is not to say the criticism is wrong because it is
familiar. For example, virtually all of the disaffected and
the disenchanted believe money to be a prerequisite for
political office. And the charges go deeper. As we see in
table 11, only a small fraction of either the disaffected or
the disenchanted are prepared to say that "elections in
this country do a good job of giving the people a real say
in what their government does."

One should sometimes dismiss a sentiment such as this
as meaningless rhetoric, as a mindless cliché of the popular culture. But the persuasiveness of such peremptory
challenges drops, I believe, as we look about the political
landscape and see the whole of it under so thick a cloud
of disillusion. Whether we speak about parties or elections, congressmen or senators, local, state, or federal
officials, executive or judiciary, or simply about "government," the alienated answer with an untiring insistence
that the political institutions of liberal democracy are
unresponsive and unrepresentative. Both the disenchanted and the disaffected declare that what citizens want and
what their congressmen care about have little to do with
each other; that Congress responds far too slowly, when

3. On this point see Jack Dennis, "Support for the Institution of Elections
by the Mass Public," *American Political Science Review* 64 (1970): 819-835.

it responds at all; in short, that the government has lost touch with the people.

The alienated speak of a government that is distant, remote, inaccessible, indifferent. The disaffected and the disenchanted agree that "those we elect to Congress in Washington lose touch with people pretty quickly" (table 12). In a similar vein they complain that a citizen cannot talk to his representatives or, if he can talk to officials, that they are unhelpful, indifferent, unresponsive. Citizens cannot count on a fair hearing; public officials care what ordinary citizens want only during elections; the government itself causes many of this country's problems. Complaints vary depending on the level and branch of government, but none escapes angry charges.

It seems as though a potpourri of emotions lies behind alienation. One can detect anger, resentment, a certain impatient concern, among others. But these feelings are blended so thoroughly that perhaps the mixture is best described as an impatient and diffuse irritation.

This irritation we can sometimes hear in the popular complaint—not a confession but a complaint—of political futility. More than three-quarters of the disaffected and the disenchanted declare that "there is almost no way people like me can have an influence on government." By contrast, equally lopsided majorities of the committed and the supportive insist that "people like me have a fair say in getting the government to do the things we care about." (See table 13.) Then, too, the disaffected and the disenchanted are equally likely to deny that almost every group has a say in the way our system of government operates; they contend, on the contrary, that "this country is really run by a small number of men at the top who only speak for a few special groups." Or, again, both the disaffected and the disenchanted are far more likely than the supportive or the committed to agree that "people like me don't

TABLE 11. THE STRUCTURE OF CYNICISM
(% DOWN – MAILBACK)

	Disaffected (N = 31)	Disenchanted (N = 41)	Middle (N = 26)	Supportive (N = 66)	Committed (N = 31)
1. (a) Most officials in government know their jobs and do them well.	41%	54%	57%	77%	90%
(b) Most people in government don't know enough to do their jobs well.	59	46	43	23	10
2. (a) Our major parties are so much alike that voters do not really get much choice when they vote.	83	64	57	43	37
(b) In most elections the parties differ enough on issues so that the voters are given a real choice.	17	46	43	57	63
3. (a) In our political system, people without money don't have much chance to get elected to public office.	93	90	63	64	41
(b) If a person has good ideas, he can usually get enough support to help him get elected.	7	10	38	36	59

4. Parties are only interested in people's votes but not in their opinions.					
(a) Agree	81	62	61	36	12
(b) Disagree	19	38	39	64	88
5. (a) Our system of elections doesn't really produce public officials who do what the people want.	82	81	50	50	30
(b) Elections in this country do a good job of giving people a real say in what their government does.	18	19	50	50	70

TABLE 12. DIFFUSENESS OF CYNICISM
(% DOWN – MAILBACK)

	Disaffected (N = 31)	Disenchanted (N = 41)	Middle (N = 26)	Supportive (N = 66)	Committed (N = 31)
1. (a) I'm pretty confident that my congressmen and senators are looking out for my interests.	17%	34%	56%	75%	89%
(b) There's not much connection between what I want and what my congressmen and senators do.	83	66	44	26	12
2. (a) Congress often fails to act on important problems even when most people favor changes.	70	80	59	42	17
(b) Congress is pretty quick to act on proposals when the majority of people favor them.	30	20	41	58	83
3. Generally speaking, those we elect to Congress in Washington lose touch with the people pretty quickly.					
(a) Agree	85	85	67	44	20
(b) Disagree	15	15	33	56	80

4. (a) Local government officials around here really listen to people's problems.	29	56	63	79	83
(b) You can talk to local officials around here but as a rule they don't pay much attention.	71	44	38	21	17
5. (a) I'm confident that government officials would give me a fair hearing if I came to them with a problem.	16	41	76	100	96
(b) If I had a problem, I doubt that I'd really get a fair hearing from a government official.	84	59	24	0	4
6. (a) Most elected public officials genuinely care about what the voters want.	16	31	48	67	77
(b) Once the election is over most public officials stop caring about what the people want.	84	69	52	33	23

Table 12 (continued)

	Disaffected (N = 31)	Disenchanted (N = 41)	Middle (N = 26)	Supportive (N = 66)	Committed (N = 31)
7. (a) Most of the government's programs over the years have worked out for the good of the country.	64	52	80	94	100
(b) When you look at the results of most government programs, they seem to have done more harm than good.	36	48	20	6	0

TABLE 13. TONE OF CYNICISM
(% DOWN – MAILBACK)

	Disaffected (N = 31)	Disenchanted (N = 41)	Middle (N = 26)	Supportive (N = 66)	Committed (N = 31)
There is almost no way people like me can have an influence on government.	81%	70%	39%	27%	23%
People like me have a fair say in getting the government to do the things we care about.	19	30	61	73	77
The way our system of government operates, almost every group has a say in running things.	15	14	50	68	77
This country is really run by a small number of men at the top who only speak for a few special groups.	85	86	50	33	23
People like me don't have any say about what the government does.					
Agree	82	51	42	29	17
Disagree	19	49	58	71	83

have any say about what the government does." In short, the alienated distinguish themselves by their readiness to complain of a lack of political influence, of their inability to make the political process responsive to their desires. Such sentiments sometimes bespeak passivity; here they are part and parcel of fired-up resentment. And the complaint of the alienated that they lack political effectiveness is just that—one more accusation against a political system they find unresponsive and unrepresentative.[4] The disenchanted, not just the disaffected, are alienated. Whatever realm of belief or feeling we look at—be it attitudes about national government, beliefs about electoral institutions of liberal democracy, opinions about the character and competence of public officials or feelings of political futility—the disenchanted earn the right to be described as cynical. We have seen occasional evidence suggesting that the disaffected may be more embittered than the disenchanted. But by any reasonable standard, the disenchanted are alienated. A chasm separates the disaffected and the disenchanted from the committed and the supportive. As the latter are allegiant, the former are alienated.

Yet are they alienated in quite the same way? Might these two sorts of alienation signify different things? As those who are overready to approve of the government are overready to yield to authority, so I expect that those who are overready to disapprove of the government are overready to confront it. In short, we shall explore the connection between balanced judgment and political protest.

4. Here I skip past an ongoing dispute over the standard efficacy items; some of them apparently tap an individual's judgment of the responsiveness of the political system rather than his own capacities to influence the outcome of the political process. See Philip E. Converse, "Public Opinion and Voting Behavior," in Fred I. Greenstein and Nelson W. Polsby, eds., *Handbook of Political Science* (Reading, Mass.: Addison-Wesley, 1975), 4: 75-170.

Political Protest and Pluralist Politics

What forms of political action may citizens properly undertake in a democratic society? Citizens may clearly do a variety of things—they may express their opinions in the name of a cause, proselytize on behalf of a candidate, make contributions, attend public meetings, cast their votes. All these forms of involvement are familiar, which is not to say that, because they are well known, all are widely engaged in or any has worn thin through use. But they are familiar because these are the ways citizens at large participate in politics, if they participate at all. Yet is this all citizen participation may amount to?

Protest: An Introductory Note

The San Francisco Bay Area has long enjoyed a reputation for political activism. How deserved, one may ask, is this reputation? In our initial survey we explored the incidence of protest. We inquired about four forms of protest: we asked respondents if they had ever participated in a peaceful protest rally or march, taken part in a sit-in, engaged in a boycott (of a store, for example) or participated in a protest that turned violent.

TABLE 14. FREQUENCY OF POLITICAL PROTEST
(BAS, N = 1,000)

	yes
Have you ever participated in a sit-in?	7%
Have you ever taken part in a boycott (of a store, for example)?	20
Have you ever taken part in a peaceful protest rally or march?	16
Have you ever taken part in a protest that turned violent?	5

Fully one in five say that they have participated in a boycott (table 14). Nearly as many—sixteen percent, to be exact—declare that they have taken part in a peaceful protest rally or march. Seven percent have participated in a sit-in, while five percent have taken part in a protest that turned violent. Plainly, a substantial number of our respondents have engaged in some form of protest. The number of protestors varies with the form of protest, ranging from a high of twenty percent to a low of five. But national polls, conducted in the same or subsequent years, help put these figures in perspective; in surveys of the country as a whole, it is difficult to turn up even a half of one percent who say they have taken part in *any* form of political protest.[5] The Bay Area, then, is an ideal locale for the study of political protest.

We asked, I should emphasize, our respondents if they had *ever* participated in these forms of protest.[6] Obviously, if we had asked them if they had taken part in a protest within the last year, or the last six months, far fewer would have given affirmative answers. We do not know *when* they participated: we can nail down their state of mind and circumstances now, but not then.

The Structure of Political Protest

My conception of protest differs from the common one. There is a tendency to look on different forms of protest as differing only in degree; I should like to suggest they may differ in kind. And the decision to look at it one way or the other cannot be made just by examining the facts of the matter.

5. Sidney Verba and Richard A. Brody, "Participation, Preferences and the War in Vietnam," *Public Opinion Quarterly* 34 (1970): 325-332.
6. The use of an extended time frame is uncommon but not novel in studies of participation: for an example of this usage, and an argument on its behalf, see Sidney Verba and Norman H. Nie, *Participation in America* (New York: Harper and Row, 1972).

It takes little imagination to conjure up reasons why we should expect to discover that all four forms of protest are positively related. For example, once a person has stopped straddling the fence between conventional and unconventional participation, and taken part in some form of protest, then the inhibitions against becoming more involved should become weaker, while the pressures to take a more active part should grow stronger. In the extreme, a person may be enveloped in a subculture of protest, a climate of opinion in which his own views, those of others and propinquity itself heighten the likelihood of engaging in various forms of protest.

Whatever the reason, the four forms of protest we inquired about are, in fact, all positively related, as table 15 shows. Quite simply, however dissimilar these types of protest may appear, they all tend to go hand in hand. The correlation coefficients between the various forms of protest are all positive and strong, with a median value of .40. The very strength of the correlations raises a further question: perhaps the four questions we asked about various forms of protest measure not four separate and distinct forms of actions, but a common propensity to protest. This is not to say that taking part in a boycott is the same thing as engaging in a violent demonstration. But it

TABLE 15. INTERRELATIONS OF FOUR
FORMS OF PROTEST
(BAS)

	Sit-in	Boycott	Peaceful protest	Violent protest
Sit-in	1.00	.21*	.41	.38
Boycott	- -	1.00	.43	.30
Peaceful protest	- -	- -	1.00	.47
Violent protest	- -	- -	- -	1.00

*Pearson product moment coefficients.

is to suggest that these different types of protest form, as it were, different steps on one staircase, that each specific form of protest reflects a common underlying predisposition to protest. A working conclusion, based on earlier studies, is that differences between one form of protest and another involve differences of degree, not of kind. As Marsh has observed:

People tend to place examples of protest behavior like demonstrations, boycotts, and occupations, and so on, along a single continuum. At one end of this continuum are mild forms of protest like signing petitions and marching peacefully, at the other end are extreme forms like deliberate damage to property and the use of personal violence. Between these extremes are ordered: demonstrations, boycotts, strikes, occupations, and similar activities.[7]

Table 16 presents the results of two models: factor analysis and classical scalogram analysis. According to the first test, there is one and only one dimension. The findings of the scalogram analysis give the same impression, until we take a second look. The coefficient of scalability is low, so low it warns us that the appearance of unidimensionality may be a statistical illusion, an artifact of the skewed numbers answering yes to these particular questions.

The findings on dimensionality, then, leave room for us to think of protest as continuous—or as discontinuous. I believe that we should distinguish two types: one is congenial to a pluralist society, the other more proble-

7. Alan Marsh, *Protest and Political Consciousness* (Beverly Hills: Sage Publications, 1977), p. 16. The other major empirical report focusing on protest is Edward N. Muller, *Aggressive Political Participation* (Princeton: Princeton University Press, 1979). The most ambitious study—Samuel H. Barnes, Max Kaase, et al., *Political Action* (Beverly Hills, Ca.: Sage, 1979)—appeared too late for use here.

TABLE 16. DIMENSIONALITY OF PROTEST
(BAS, N = 1,000)

	Factor analysis (oblique rotation)
Sit-in	.682
Boycott	.643
Peaceful protest	.817
Violent protest	.751

	Scalogram analysis
Coefficient of reproducibility	.9481
Minimum marginal reproducibility	.8785
Percent improvement	.0696
Coefficient of scalability	.5726

Eigenvalue: 2:109. Proportion of total communality accounted for by factor: .527. Oblique rotation: The structure is the same, whatever the method of rotation.

matic. One type of protest is in manner combative, disruptive, provocative, aggressive. I shall call this adversary protest. Under this heading fall sit-ins and violent demonstrations. The other type of protest may be argumentative but it is not combative. I shall call this advocacy protest. Under this heading fall boycotting and peaceful demonstrations.

Advocacy protest is a form of political action to call public attention to a social wrong, to demonstrate the sincerity of one's convictions, to persuade by one's actions and arguments one's fellow citizens—including public officials—to join in redressing an injustice. To lump advocacy protest with all other types of unconventional protest is to miss an important point. As Muller has remarked:

Peaceful rallies or marches, though unconventional, are nevertheless similar to electoral participation in that both involve "within system" behavior which does not challenge the authority of the state—hence both are essentially conformative in nature.[8]

On balance, I find the distinction between advocacy and adversary protest reasonable in a world where few things are clear cut. It contrasts forms of political action which are coercive and those which are not. On this point sit-ins, perhaps the most troubling example of adversary protest, may prove the most instructive. Wolfinger and his colleagues underline the coercive character of sit-ins when they observe:

The logic of nonviolent physical coercion is that whoever gets their foot in the doorway first decides who gets to enter and leave, even if there are only 25 people blocking the door and 200 waiting to get in or out.[9]

One might say that all forms of protest aim to be persuasive; they just differ in whom they set out to persuade and how they go about doing it. Certainly the difference between advocacy and adversary protest cannot be reduced to a question of being committed to an idea, nor even to the question of whether one's actions serve as public advertisement of that commitment. Nor can we say that it is an attempt at justification, during or immediately after the act of protest, that distinguishes advocacy from adversary protest. Those taking part in violent demonstrations have gone to great lengths on occasion to justify their actions. Rather what marks advocacy protest is the attempt to persuade others, *in terms of what they already believe is right and proper*, that they, too, should join in the effort to redress some wrong.

8. Edward N. Muller, "A Test of a Partial Theory of Potential for Political Violence," *American Political Science Review* 66 (1972): 928-959.

9. Raymond E. Wolfinger, Martin Shapiro and Fred I. Greenstein, *Dynamics of American Politics* (Englewood Cliffs, N.J.: Prentice-Hall, 1976), p. 572.

A remark or two about what this distinction passes over may help make clear what it centers on. To begin with, the distinction between these two types of protest does not hinge on the issue of civil disobedience. I take civil disobedience to be a form of political action employed to test the validity of a law. That criterion may or may not apply to any particular instance of advocacy *or* adversary protest. Nor do I take the distinction between the two types of protest to run precisely parallel to violent and nonviolent, or even legal and illegal. Adversary protest may be nonviolent and yet coercive; witness the case of sit-ins. Moreover, a peaceful rally, failing to win some minor permit withheld by a willful official, might then be an illegal act; I would consider it an example of advocacy protest nonetheless.

Second, the distinction turns on a difference in manner, not motive. It is tempting to answer that the crucial point of divergence between these two types of protest lies in the motives behind them, the objectives being sought; and, indeed, in some sense or other of these words, that surely must be so. Nonetheless, we cannot advance this sort of argument *as a basis for drawing this distinction between these two types of protest in the first place.* We know too little. We know what people have done, but not when, under what circumstances or for what reasons. The relation between belief and behavior is complex and contingent in general, and surely no less so in the case of political protest. Thus a person may join a peaceful demonstration to satisfy his curiosity, to express his convictions, to impress his friends or for any of a variety of other reasons. For that matter, there is much that is fortuitous. A person may find himself joining in because quite by chance he happened to be on the spot in the company of others who joined in for their own reasons. Or, as must be the case for a number of respondents, a person may join what he has at the outset every reason to believe will be a peaceful demonstration but which turns into a violent one because of the actions of others.

By an "advocate," then, I mean one who has taken part in a boycott or a peaceful demonstration, or both—but who has eschewed any other form of protest. By an "adversary" I mean one who has taken part in a sit-in or a violent demonstration, or both, whatever other forms of protest he has participated in. Whether a person proves to be one or the other, I believe, depends heavily on whether his judgment is balanced or not; but before taking this up, I should like to suggest why distinguishing these two types of protest may be more broadly instructive.

A Second Revolution in Participation

The first revolution in participation in America got under way against restrictions on the suffrage in the late eighteenth century. It ran for nearly two centuries, culminating in the Civil Rights Act of 1965. The story of this revolution centers on who could participate. As this revolution has unfolded we have witnessed an enormous extension of the role of citizenship in America as once-proscribed groups—above all, women and blacks—have been added to the roll of eligible voters.

A second revolution may be in the making. Its concern is not who counts as a participant but what counts as participation. What a citizen could and should do in politics was once well understood. He might contribute money to a political party, a candidate or a cause; attempt to sway the votes of his friends or neighbors, attend an election rally or pitch in as a volunteer worker in a political campaign; wear a button, plant a sign in his front lawn or put a sticker on his car bumper on behalf of a candidate or issue; or even attempt to run for office. Of course, there were other things a citizen might say or do.

He might rail at a local official in order to get a street repaired, or attend the local school board meeting to vent a grievance. But political participation was, by and large, electoral participation. The 1960s brought a call for citizens to go beyond the ballot box. The arguments over protest—the questions about its role in a pluralistic society—go to the limits of citizen action in a democratic polity. So intertwined in our thought are the ideas of citizenship and elections that many draw, sometimes without intending to, an invidious line between conventional and unconventional participation. The conventional embraces the familiar and acceptable; the unconventional, the unfamiliar and the problematic. Conventional participation was synonymous with electoral involvement; unconventional participation, with protest.[10] But what is acceptable—what citizens will do, and not merely endorse—can change.

Profiles
All stereotypes are not all wrong. The stereotype of a protestor depicts a person who is young, in his late teens or early twenties, well educated, typically a college student or a college dropout, whose parents are well-to-do. This stereotype has a considerable measure of truth—for one style of protest. In the Bay Area Sample, fully forty percent of those who have engaged in adversary protest—adversaries, as I shall call them—hold at least a B.A., compared with only seventeen percent of those who have never engaged in any act of protest (see table 17). Advocates, as I shall call our second group of protestors, are also well educated. But though both types differ from our

10. It would be a mistake, however, to consider political protest as the rule, or even the chief form that the impulse to extend the idea of citizenship assumed. On the enlargement of participation in industrial politics see Robert A. Dahl, *After the Revolution* (New Haven: Yale University Press, 1970).

TABLE 17. DEMOGRAPHIC CHARACTERISTICS
OF PROTESTORS
(% DOWN – BAS)

	Non-protestors (N = 723)	Advocates (N = 187)	Adversaries (N = 90)
Education:			
0-8th grade	13%	4%	1%
Some high school	15	7	3
High school graduate	34	30	25
Some college	22	17	32
College graduate and above	17	42	40
Age:			
18-21 years	4	5	18
22-26 years	10	24	40
27-30 years	8	15	8
31-39 years	19	17	21
40-49 years	18	19	8
50-59 years	16	14	4
60 years and over	25	6	1
Income:			
$0-4,999	18	11	31
$5,000-9,999	31	20	29
$10,000-14,999	25	31	22
$15,000 and above	27	38	18
Social class (self-designation):			
Upper middle	16	19	13
Middle	49	55	38
Working and lower	35	27	50
Occupation:			
Cleaning private household, laborers	9	6	10
Personal service, food service operatives	16	11	7
Health service, transport mechanics, repairmen	7	7	9
Protective, craftsmen	7	7	6

Table 17 (*continued*)

Clerical, executive secretaries, sales, professional nurses, health	25	24	27
Secretaries, managers, administrators, technicians, writers, professional religious	23	22	21
Professional, technical and other	11	24	20

third group, the nonprotestors, they differ from each other, too. Advocates and adversaries apparently represent different social constituencies. Adversaries are nearly twice as likely as advocates to have begun but not yet finished college. The reason for this difference comes quickly to mind—age. As the table shows, advocates are substantially older than adversaries. Nearly sixty percent of those who have engaged in adversary protest are in their mid-twenties or younger, whereas only thirty percent of those who have engaged in advocacy protest are in that age group. Conversely, nearly forty percent of the advocates are forty years old, or older, compared with just thirteen percent of the adversaries.

In terms of their age, the similarity of advocates and nonprotestors stands out. There is an occasional point of difference—for example, in the proportion who are in their twenties or in their sixties or older. But they are very much alike. The proportion of each in their teens, thirties, forties or fifties is nearly identical (table 17).

The appeal of adversary protest is restricted and distinctive, that of advocacy protest broader and more various. Most notably, advocacy protest enlists substantial numbers in their thirties, forties and fifties. Advocates are better off than citizens at large, but not by much. All in all, the two are much alike—and quite unlike those who have taken part in adversary protest. Adversaries are nearly three times as likely as advocates to have earned $5,000 or less; conversely, advocates are twice as likely as adversaries to have earned $15,000 or more. Of course, the difference with regard to income dovetails with the differences with regard to education and age. Looking at these three groups, we see that two are quite similar and one is quite dissimilar. The advocate looks very much like the citizen at large. It is not, I should add, as though he falls at some hypothetical midpoint between those who will have no part of protest and those who commit themselves to the most combative forms of protest. Advocates enjoy some advantages which facilitate all forms of participation—above all, in education. Yet all in all, advocacy protest is a style of action which is inclusive, demographically at any rate; it draws broadly, if not heavily, on the portion of the larger community that takes an active interest in politics. The clientele for this type of protest is not drawn overwhelmingly from one demiclass—the college-age young, as is that for adversary protest. Advocacy protest has won a wider constituency.

Advocates, to be sure, are far more liberal in outlook than those who eschew all forms of protest, though less liberal than adversaries (table 18). But it is not so much the gross differences *between* groups that I find suggestive—the outcome is much as anyone would expect—as it is the differences *within* groups. Consider the variation in views, the extent to which each of these groups embraces the spectrum of opinion. Every major stance finds substantial representation among advocates: half are liberal in some degree, nearly a third moderates, and a fifth conservative.[11] In contrast, adversaries include only a

11. The index of liberalism-conservatism, devised by Herbert McClosky, was constructed by summing scores obtained on five items, given in Appendix B; scoring and coding details are also to be found there. I might suggest the

TABLE 18. POLITICAL OUTLOOK AND PROTEST
(% DOWN – BAS)

	Non-protestors (N = 723)	Advocates (N = 187)	Adversaries (N = 90)
Lib-con attitude index:			
Strong liberal	5%	26%	40%
Liberal	13	24	29
Middle-of-the-road	31	30	22
Conservative	26	11	3
Strong conservative	26	10	4
Party identification:			
Republican	27	8	2
Independent	21	24	51
Democrat	52	69	47
Ideology (self-identification):			
Radical	1	6	19
Liberal	18	50	43
Middle-of-the-road	53	29	27
Conservative	24	8	9
Strong conservative	4	0	2

sprinkling of conservatives while nonprotestors include only a handful of the very liberal. That advocacy protest should win so substantial a constituency among the political center and, as impressively, among conservatives testifies to its broad appeal. The partisan sympathies of advocates do give the impression of a group that is more restrictive. If we compare the party loyalties of advocates and nonprotestors, we can see that the former are predominantly Democratic in sympathy, with no more than a token number of Republicans. It is tempting to

manifest content of the measure by noting that the questions covered such topics as the leniency of courts, the degree of equality that obtains and the responsibility of the wealthy for the condition of the poor.

take this as evidence that the reach of advocacy protest extends only to a partisan pocket of society. But this is not to say that the appeal of this style of protest is limited to a narrow segment, or to a segment which in political temper and tone is at odds with the larger community. The converse is the case. Democratic sympathies are the rule, Republican ones the exception. In the Bay Area sample, twice as many identify with the Democratic as the Republican party. To be a Democrat is the norm, and emphatically so in social circles concerned with the divisive issues of the late sixties. Advocates exemplify the prevailing norms, albeit in a heightened fashion.

It is adversaries who stand apart from the established pattern of partisan commitments of the larger community. Half of the adversaries are pure independents, denying any measure of identification with either party. It would be an exaggeration to say that adversaries have severed all ties with the established parties of the party system. But they surely do depart from the dominant norms of partisan identification. And again we see in yet another respect that the difference between adversaries and advocates overshadows any difference between advocates and citizens at large.

In sum, what stands out is less the difference *between* protestors and nonprotestors and more the difference *within* protestors. One style of protest enjoys a broad and inclusive constituency. To characterize advocacy protestors as middle-class and middle-aged would be to miss much of the point. Advocacy protest, unlike adversary protest, appeals to people in various strata, from diverse backgrounds, with disparate political outlooks. Advocates are not a mirror of the larger community. But with the exception only of partisanship, their ranks take in a remarkably various and inclusive assortment of individuals drawn from throughout the larger community, not just one narrow segment of it.

Conventional versus Unconventional Participation

Does political protest—and, above all, adversary protest—represent an alternative to more conventional forms of citizen participation? Do people turn to unconventional forms of political action because they have given up on the conventional? How we answer these questions has much to do with whether we think there has been some enlargement of the ideal of citizenship. We may have witnessed an extension of the limits of citizen action —a pushing back of the boundaries of what citizens may do—or a repudiation by protestors of the more traditional aspects of the citizen's role.

The answer may seem straightforward. Table 19 presents the relationship between various types of protest and a number of forms of conventional participation. Quite simply, protestors, adversaries as well as advocates, take part in conventional politics. Moreover, both adversaries and advocates are more likely to participate than nonprotestors. For example, two-thirds of those who have protested report that they have talked or written to someone in government about official matters, compared with little better than thirty percent of those who have not engaged in any form of protest. Finally, protestors are more likely to be active in every form of conventional politics—or, at any rate, in every form we inquired about. To be sure, this depends somewhat on the form of participation. By and large, protestors and nonprotestors are most likely to differ on forms of involvement which place a premium on individual initiative, that is, on personal spontaneity and assertiveness. Two examples: contacting a government official and

TABLE 19. CONVENTIONAL PARTICIPATION
(% DOWN − BAS)

	Non-protestors (N = 723)	Advocates (N = 187)	Adversaries (N = 90)
	Percentage responding yes		
Have you ever talked to or written to someone in government about official matters?	34%	69%	66%
Have you ever signed a complaint or petition about some political issue?	48	80	90
Have you ever worked for a political party or a candidate?	17	48	36
As you know, most people vote; did you vote in the last California primary election?*	62	73	62

*The percentages responding yes are enormously inflated − a caution to bear in mind for the other figures, too.

working on behalf of a political party or candidate. As the form of participation becomes more routinized, the differences between protestors and nonprotestors becomes smaller, and in the paradigmatic case of voting vanish, or virtually so. Those who engage in advocacy protest are only slightly more likely than those who eschew protest to report voting in the last California primary, while those who engage in adversary protest are neither more nor less likely than nonprotestors to report voting.[12]

12. Estimates of participation tend to exaggeration, though these are even more exaggerated than normal, as I have warned in the table. For a recent and especially thoughtful review of the research on various forms of participation see Richard A. Brody, "The Puzzle of Political Participation in America," in Anthony King, ed., The New American Political System (Washington: American Enterprise Institute, 1978), pp. 287-324.

Do these findings disprove the notion that these two modes of participation—unconventional and conventional—are mutually repellent, if not mutually exclusive? We cannot decide this question with these data. The matter of timing is all important. We know what a person has done—to the extent that we take him at his word. We do not know *when* he has done it. A person may once have been extraordinarily active in all forms of conventional citizen politics, only to abandon them in exasperated frustration, and, as a consequence, turn all his energies to unconventional politics; or vice versa.

The problem goes further. By normal or conventional participation, we mean chiefly electoral politics. When we speak of this sort of political participation, we have in mind such things as turning out to vote, canvassing friends and neighbors on behalf of a candidate, attending campaign meetings, donating money to a candidate or a cause. By and large, these are the kinds of things most citizens are most likely to do when a campaign is under way. To be sure, citizens participate between elections. I mean only to remark the obvious: much of what we think of as conventional participation takes place periodically, on schedule, at definite and prescribed intervals.

Political protest, by contrast, operates on a different calendar. There are seasons of protest. But protest of whatever type, whether advocacy or adversary in nature, is not institutionalized. Political protests are in some respects rather more like earthquakes than elections. The first two involve unexpected, if inevitable, eruptions. We can predict well the day of an election; we can do no more than worry about an upheaval.

To put the point more exactly, any person facing an opportunity to participate in conventional politics is unlikely to know that he may quite shortly be presented with an opportunity to participate in unconventional politics. But only when a person is presented with both alternatives can he be said to choose one to the exclusion of the other. People may feel that they have made such a choice, even when they have not; they may report that they have given up on conventional politics because it doesn't work, or that they have turned their backs on unconventional politics because it is futile. Citizens are in a position to choose between conventional and unconventional politics only rarely—and then only briefly.

Alienation and Protest

Alienation is a spur to protest. The evidence consistently shows a relationship between the two. But there is something about declaring that the two are related that is, or should be, discomfiting. For our working conception of alienation is providentially narrow and broad. When we speak of alienation, we take care to mean *political* alienation—that is, pronounced dissatisfaction with political institutions and policies. Just as frustration need not lead to aggression,[13] alienation need not lead to political protest—and likely will not, if by alienation we mean the whole spectrum of discontent, personal and social as well as political. Dissatisfaction is likely to affect political belief and behavior, to the degree discontent is politicized. The impact of dissatisfaction is likely to be registered in the political realm only to the extent people see a connection between the grievances they suffer from and the political order they live under.[14] But if our conception of alienation is in one respect narrow, it is in another conveniently broad. Studies of political protest and violence

13. Marsh takes up this question from the perspective of a psychologist studying politics. See *Protest*, pp. 133-163.
14. For two attempts to specify empirically this connection see Paul M. Sniderman and Richard A. Brody, "Coping: The Ethic of Self-Reliance," *American Journal of Political Science* 21 (1977): 501-521, and Brody and Sniderman, "From Life Space to Polling Place: The Relevance of Personal Concerns for Voting Behavior," *British Journal of Political Science* 7 (1977): 337-360.

have shown that a variety of forces lie behind oppositional politics, including relative deprivation, status anxieties, a sense of control of one's own life, to mention a few. These feelings of resentment, anger, grievance, deprivation and the like seem to run together. So when we study one, say political alienation, we may take advantage of a form of shorthand and see the joint effect of a great number of other sentiments, too.

The decisive question, then, is not *whether* alienation and protest are related. It is learning *how* the two are related that matters.[15] I want to turn attention from the fact to the form of the relationship. As people grow more alienated, are they more likely to protest? Or must they, perhaps, become alienated in a particular way?

The established approach in the assessment of protest, as in the measurement of alienation, is to proceed as though it were a continuous variable. Individuals are rank-ordered along a single continuum or, in Marsh's phrase, a "corridor of protest," according to how frequently they have engaged in various forms of protest. Figure 2 illustrates the expected form of the relation between alienation and protest, so conceived.

In the usual view of things, we should expect that the more alienated are more prone to protest; and, of course, this is why figure 2 shows the relation between the two to be monotonic. This representation is no whimsy; all the empirical findings to date—including those reported from these very data—suggest that there is a positive and impressively strong correlation between alienation and protest. Yet it seems to me reasonable to ask whether our recognizing that there is a distinction between two types of alienation will alter our appreciation of the connection between discontent and protest in a pluralist society.

A lack of balance in judgment suggests a lack of re-

15. Thoughtful students of protest, Marsh and Muller, for example, have recognized and underscored this very point.

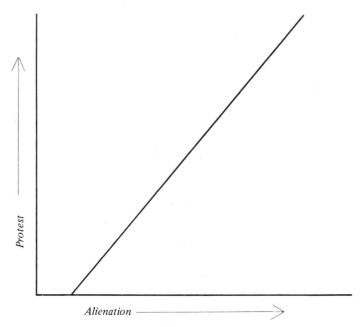

FIG. 2. EXPECTED FORM OF THE RELATIONSHIP BETWEEN
ALIENATION AND PROTEST.

straint. It bespeaks an impulsivity, a disinclination to
deliberate and to be deliberate. It signals the politics of
enthusiasm. Politics knows enthusiasts of disbelief as well
as of belief. For the embittered may be enthusiasts, too.
The disaffected as well as the committed are people of
excessive zeal. And as the committed are overready to
side with authority, the disaffected are overready to confront it.

What form specifically should the relation between
alienation and protest take? There are two predictions:

1. The disaffected—and to a lesser degree, the disenchanted—should prove more likely to protest than
other citizens.

2. The disaffected should prove most likely to take

part in adversary protest, *but the disenchanted should prove neither more nor less likely than other citizens generally to engage in adversary protest.* The first prediction is straightforward and a safe bet. The second is less obvious and more important, and so merits a word or two. To the degree the disenchanted are given to deliberation, they should be more deliberate. Compared with the disaffected, they should be more averse to pitching themselves into protest. Above all, the disenchanted should eschew adversary forms of protest. Adversary protest, after all, entails undisguised opposition to authorities. And for that reason I expect the disenchanted to repudiate it.

Both expectations are handsomely confirmed. To take the first prediction first, the disaffected are far and away the most likely to have protested (see table 20). Almost six in every ten of the disaffected have engaged in some form of protest. Moreover, the disenchanted are substantially more likely than the ordinary citizen to have protested, though they are understandably less likely to have done so than the disaffected. In short, we fare well on our first prediction, though admittedly this does not carry us far. For the crux of the argument is that the disaffected and the disenchanted should part company when it comes to adversary protest.

The findings are impressive. Figure 3 illustrates the proportions engaging in adversary protest among the disaffected, the disenchanted, the middle, the supportive and the committed. Not surprisingly, the disaffected lead the parade. Nearly a third of them have taken part in some form of adversary protest. But what is remarkable is the drop-off between the disaffected and the disenchanted. In figure 3, the line tracing the proportion of adversaries is at its height among the disaffected, and then plummets: only about five percent of the disenchanted have ever taken

TABLE 20. ALIENATION AND PROTEST
(% DOWN – BAS)

	Disaffected (N = 171)	Disenchanted (N = 193)	Middle (N = 154)	Supportive (N = 256)	Committed (N = 226)
Participation in Protest:					
Nonprotestors	43%	62%	76%	80%	92%
Protestors	58	38	25	20	8

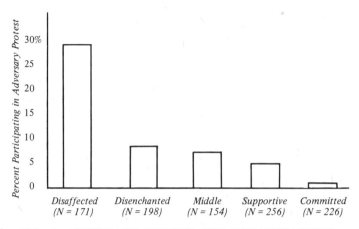

FIG. 3. ADVERSARY PROTEST AND DISSATISFACTION (BAY AREA SURVEY).

part in adversary protest. And the curve continues on, describing virtually a straight line, neither rising nor falling, at least until the very end. The disenchanted are no more likely to take part in adversary protest than are citizens at large—including the supportive, who are manifestly allegiant and at the opposite end of the spectrum of alienation.

Profiles

Who are the disaffected? How do they differ from the disenchanted, or, for that matter, from the supportive or the committed? Now that we know the distinctions among them make a difference politically, we need to know something of what these people are like, an approximate description of their social background and circumstances.

Table 21 presents the relations between varieties of alienation and age and education, respectively. The two extremes differ: forty-four percent of the disaffected are thirty or younger, half the committed are fifty or older.

TABLE 21. DEMOGRAPHIC CHARACTERISTICS OF DISAFFECTION AND DISENCHANTMENT
(% DOWN – BAS)

	Disaffected (N = 171)	Disenchanted (N = 193)	Middle (N = 194)	Supportive (N = 256)	Committed (N = 226)
Age:					
18-21 years	10%	5%	6%	5%	3%
22-26 years	22	17	10	19	7
27-30 years	12	12	9	8	5
31-39 years	25	20	12	20	18
40-49 years	12	17	23	17	17
50-59 years	10	16	16	14	17
60 years and over	9	14	24	17	34
Education:					
0-8th grade	9	8	14	6	16
Some high school	10	10	21	9	14
High school graduate	29	31	35	32	36
Some college	21	24	17	28	16
College graduate and above	32	26	13	27	18

The disenchanted and the supportive, however, do not differ. The committed are more poorly educated than the others, but the supportive are as well educated as the disenchanted or the disaffected. It is necessary to look at people who are similar in age to see that the alienated may in fact be dissimilar in schooling. In brief, among the young the disaffected are more likely than the disenchanted to have completed college; and, astonishingly, the committed are at least as likely as the supportive to have finished college (table 22). To put the point squarely, the two extreme positions are poles attracting the comparatively well educated who were young and presumably impressionable in the 1960s. The picture differs for those who are older and who were presumably less malleable when they first heard the clamorous issues of the 1960s. The disenchanted are, if anything, better educated than the disaffected. And, as we should expect, the committed are substantially less well educated than the supportive.[16] The young and the old are led, albeit by somewhat different paths, to a common end—a susceptibility to one-sided orientations toward government, whether zealously for or against.

The role of political protest in a pluralist society is the question before us. I have spoken of varieties of alienation and of protest and of the distinctiveness of their connections. I should like to note now some complexities.

Advocacy Protest and Reciprocal Restraints

Citizens engaging in advocacy protest impose upon themselves restraints that those engaging in adversary

16. These findings should be kept in mind when reading the following chapter; a number of rival interpretations that may occur to a reader will founder on them. The fact that the supportive and the disenchanted are so very

TABLE 22. THE DISAFFECTED AND THE DISENCHANTED, EXTENT
OF EDUCATION, BY AGE

(% DOWN – BAS)

Education	Disaffected (N = 96)	Disenchanted (N = 80)	Middle (N = 46)	Supportive (N = 100)	Committed (N = 51)
Under age 35 years:					
0-8th grade*	—	—	4%	—	4%
Some high school	9%	9%	20	10%	7
High school graduate	28	40	38	36	37
Some college	21	22	31	30	19
College graduate and above	41	29	7	23	33
	(N = 75)	(N = 113)	(N = 148)	(N = 156)	(N = 175)
Age 35 years and above:					
0-8th grade	21	14	18	8	20
Some high school	10	10	21	8	16
High school graduate	30	25	34	29	36
Some college	20	26	12	26	15
College graduate and above	19	25	16	29	13

*Where no figures are given, the proportion was less than 1 percent.

protest do not. For example, citizens conducting a boy-cott as a rule make it their practice—indeed, they charac-teristically make it a matter of principle—to eschew force, or the threat of force. In contrast, in a demonstration that turns violent, participants as a rule have not made in advance thorough and public preparations to rule out violence. This is not to say that they always, or even usually, have consciously committed themselves to vio-lence; I mean to say only that they have not consciously and publicly committed themselves *against* it. And it is in this sense that advocacy protest entails self-imposed re-straints that adversary protest does not.

Those who impose restraints on themselves may there-by impose restraints on the state, and for at least two reasons. First, the more likely a protest is to involve force, or the threat of force, the more likely authorities are to respond with force, or a show of force—which may be all it takes to ignite a combustible situation. Second, advo-cacy protestors, by disavowing force or the threat of force, publicly place themselves in a weaker position vis-à-vis the authorities. It is not only that they pose no immediate threat to order; they plainly are in no position to resist force, should authorities choose to exercise it.

In a pluralist society the weakness of advocacy protest may be a part of its strength. In social life, the strong do not always exploit the weak; they tend not to take full advantage of their strength, for example, when doing so would cost them the good opinion of others whose opinion matters to them.[17] A pluralist society affords a variety of audiences—including elite audiences—and a measure of

different in their social circumstances throws into even bolder relief the fact that they are similar in their habits of mind. And the same argument holds true, with perhaps even greater force, for the committed and the disaffected.

17. William J. Goode, *The Celebration of Heroes* (Berkeley: University of California Press, 1978), p. 333.

access to them. In the political life of a democratic society authorities often cannot exploit their strength without restraint, precisely because advocacy protestors make such a public point of their weakness. A fight between one party which disavows force and another party which resorts to it is not a fair fight, and will be so perceived by others whose good opinion is valued. So by imposing restraints on themselves protestors may impose restraints on authorities.

Such restraints are not guaranteed to inhibit the use of force by authorities. The history of the civil rights movement in the South in the early 1960s testifies to the readiness of local authorities, backed by local support, to break these restraints, and the reluctance of certain national agencies, notably the FBI, to intercede. But the movement is in part a history of the self-defeating consequences of flaunting such restraints by authorities. The sight of snarling dogs snapping at children and of police herding marchers with electric cattle prods outraged citizens at large and political leaders; and, as a result, both very likely gave their support to the protestors more abundantly than they otherwise would have done.

Clear violation of restraint by authorities, then, may redound to the advantage of protestors.[18] And, to the degree authorities learn this lesson, advocacy protest establishes a set of reciprocal restraints. By imposing restraints on themselves, protestors impose restraints on authorities. Strong forms of protest—for example, riots—can be readily crushed in a pluralist society. In contrast, weak forms of protest—that is, forms that involve restraint—cannot be dealt with so summarily.

18. This boomerang effect is, I suspect, not very robust. For example, it is unlikely to occur if a form of protest is unfamiliar or involves a threat of force, even should the authorities employ excessive force.

Violence: Risk versus Threat

It is tempting to base the distinction between adversary and advocacy protest on the issue of violence. Plainly, adversary protest involves a form of action which all parties—protestors, authorities and onlookers—take to be oppositional. Moreover, the spirit of the action is aggressive: adversary protestors assume the role of antagonist, not advocate; and as antagonists their manner is combative. It may seem, therefore, reasonable to say that adversary protest carries with it a threat of violence that advocacy protest does not. But as Marsh rightly remarks, most forms of political protest carry with them a risk of violence, whether or not they attempt to raise or rule out a threat of violence.[19] Marchers in a large demonstration require the cooperation, or at least the neutrality, of spectators and authorities. Failing the good conduct of either onlookers or officials, advocacy protest may lead to violence, however benign the original intentions. Protest of whatever style involves forms of action that are unfamiliar and therefore threatening. For protest to draw attention it must be out of the ordinary. And partly because it is extraordinary, citizens at large look on it with suspicion and hostility—even before the protests have occurred and the protestors have had a chance to present their case.[20]

Protest may set off a public backlash. But the danger is not so much that protest may be counterproductive; it is rather that public reaction to it may reward official excess. The experience of the 1968 Democratic Convention may teach more than one lesson. But is it unreasonable to

19. Marsh, *Protest*, p. 15.
20. For a look at a variety of findings on attitudes toward civil rights demonstrations, the effectiveness of such forms of protest as sit-ins and peaceful demonstrations and the causes of racial unrest see Hazel Erskine, "The Polls: Demonstrations & Race Riots," *Public Opinion Quarterly* 31 (1967-68): 655-677.

wonder whether the public approval of the conduct of police and other officials may not only teach authorities that they can get away with objectionable acts, but also that they may even be honored for them? And might this not encourage authorities to think that they can and should do it again?

The point, I should emphasize, is not the malignant intent of the authorities; it is their circumstances more than their aims that concern me. The position of authorities places them under the pressure of civic approval to break the restraints of civil authority. Authorities may be beset by protests of all varieties, all of which carry a risk of violence. The more unremitting the barrage authorities must face in their everyday work, the greater the chances they will acquire a siege mentality. Yet though besieged, they are not beleaguered. Is the public not clamorous in its support? And it is when authorities are beset by protestors and backed by citizens that they are especially likely to overstep their powers in a pluralist society.

Justification: A Threshold Problem

Plainly, adversary protest may raise problems for a pluralist society. But so may advocacy protest. Specifically, I want to discuss the question of justifying protest, of persuading people that it is reasonable and right to perform some act of protest, not because this is the only question but because it raises perhaps the most often overlooked problem.

To see where the problem lies, consider the relation between advocacy protest and civil disobedience. The concept of civil disobedience is intimidatingly complicated; and if we attempt to pin down the vagaries of its meaning, we shall sink in the attempt. So let me offer an example of what I take civil disobedience to mean for the purpose at hand—the civil rights sit-ins of the early 1960s.

Civil disobedience, so understood, is seemingly a species of advocacy protest. It works to spotlight a grievous wrong and thereby to awake the moral conscience of the larger community. Yet civil disobedience is unlike the forms of advocacy protest we have examined in this study in at least one respect: it involves breaking the law, while boycotting and peaceful demonstrations are, or are seen to be, legal.

Armies of commentators have clashed over the question of when civil disobedience is justified in a democratic society, largely because this form of citizen action involves deliberate violation of law. Yet other species of advocacy protest may present more formidable problems precisely because they need not entail breaking a law.

In general, the more difficult or forbidding an action, the stronger or more compelling a justification it requires, if substantial numbers are to perform that act. So civil disobedience requires a strong justification, if only because a law will be broken. We cannot assess the strength of such a justification in any absolute sense. Moreover, the amount of justification a particular act requires may change with time and experience; so it likely takes less as the act becomes more familiar and perhaps even fashionable. Yet it seems reasonable to think of justification as a hurdle: the stronger the justification an action requires, the higher the hurdle it presents. Not surprisingly, the number of people who will jump a hurdle and the number of times they will do it depends on the height of the hurdle.

Precisely because we think of advocacy protest as less extreme, demanding or risky, the hurdle it presents is lower and so more readily jumped. And to the extent that advocacy protest is easier to resort to than civil disobedience, the chances increase that people will resort to advocacy protest in a situation where it does more harm than good, or that they will resort to it so often that it more frequently does more harm than good, or yet again, that it loses its capacity to do good, whether or not it does harm. It may seem odd to speak of harm in this context, for advocacy protest owes its appeal in part to its apparent innocuousness. It seems to be a style of citizen action which promises sizable benefits at little cost either to those who take part or to the larger society. And quite apart from its utility as a way of redressing social grievances, some would argue on behalf of advocacy protest on the larger ground that it represents a more active citizenry. In a democracy, they would argue, participation is a good in itself, and, in this view, the adoption of advocacy forms of protest by a broad and inclusive constituency reflects an enlargement of the idea of citizenship.

Yet just because advocacy protest seems unlikely to do harm, it may in the end prove harmful. The chief reason people turn to it is a reason for worrying about it. It takes far less to persuade people to join in a boycott than to persuade them to break a law. But a boycott can do great damage, and can do so on behalf of values that are noxious to the standards of a democratic society. It is one thing to stand by and watch a boycott of a huge chain of grocery stores; it is quite another to watch a white boycott crush a small black co-op in the South.

I mean to give more than the wary warning that advocacy protest is a weapon, and like all weapons can hurt as well as help. My point is twofold. First, advocacy protest is a weapon within easy reach, compared with other forms of protest. Second, advocacy protest is a majority strategy. Of course, it is an active few, not the many, who spearhead this form of protest. But advocacy protest is, above all, a strategy of appeal to majority sentiment, a way of persuading people that an issue matters in the light of the *established* standards of the larger community. Advocacy protest is an application of the majority principle to meet, and to circumscribe, minority grievances.

The Spiral Problem

Success threatens to spell the failure of advocacy protest. Since the argument is a familiar one, I shall spend only a word or two outlining it. Advocacy protest faces a dilemma. To be effective, it must excite attention and win the approval of others—including as a rule the politically involved and influential—by successfully appealing to their moral sensibilities. But the more success such a strategy enjoys, the more likely it is to be imitated, and in the process routinized.

The more readily citizens resort to protest, the less distinct becomes the boundary between advocacy and adversary protest. An eloquent speech, a solitary march, a midnight vigil, once on the front page, is pushed to the back. No longer as novel, it is no longer as newsworthy. A variety of factors is at work—a mounting frustration, an expansion of objectives, the pressure of internal and external demands on protest groups—but the net effect favors an increasingly militant, dramatic and aggressive style of protest. In the process more than a few protestors and protest groups are swept over the spidery line between advocacy and adversary protest.

An oversimplification. There are obviously some mechanisms of social control that effectively check or channel oppositional politics. But forms of protest do compete for support. And in this competition adversary protest tends to undercut the appeal of advocacy protest, both within and outside the ranks of protestors. On the one side, advocacy protest appears increasingly futile; on the other side, the more protestors appear as adversaries, the more they lose the quality that makes protest success-ful in the first place—the ability to appeal persuasively to the moral sensibilities of citizens at large and especial-ly elites.

The Distinction between Advocacy and Adversary Protest

The notion of a built-in spiral raises the question of whether we should distinguish between advocacy and ad-versary style. I have no direct evidence of such an incli-nation to escalation. But at least one of the findings should give pause to anyone attempting to argue that advocacy and adversary protest are in fact separate and distinct styles of action.

When we first looked at the four specific forms of protest—boycotting, peaceful demonstrations, sit-ins and demonstrations that turned violent—we saw that all are positively and strongly interrelated. Perhaps even more to the point, these forms of protest are hierarchically ordered. Those who have taken part in the more difficult kinds of protest have also taken part in the less difficult; those who have engaged in adversary protest are over-whelmingly likely to have engaged in advocacy pro-test, too.

What should we make of this? At one extreme, it ap-pears folly to argue that involvement with milder forms of protest leads with hypnotic inevitability to involve-ment with stronger forms. At the other extreme, it ap-pears bullheaded to deny not only that various kinds of protest are related, but that they may be related in this very particular way. Unhappily, with the data at hand we cannot say anything with assurance about any path an individual may follow over time from advocacy to adversary protest. We do not lack for anecdotal evidence, reports firsthand or otherwise of people who found themselves committed to militant forms of protest after, and apparently as a consequence of, involvement with milder forms of protest. No doubt, there is something to be said for some notion of recruitment. But since it may take so many disparate forms, and our data do not permit us to establish even so primitive an issue as who did what when, I should like to offer only one remark.

Broadly speaking, the very qualities that recommend advocacy protest—its earnestness of purpose, its suasive rather than combative manner, its self-imposed restraint —may, ironically, contribute to a climate of opinion hostile to the spirit of democratic politics. As the resort to protest becomes more indiscriminate, less exacting, more promiscuous, the politics of protest is likely to become more intolerant, mean-spirited, divisive. By legitimizing one type of protest, advocacy protest may legitimize the idea of protest itself.

Yet there are limits. What are the boundaries of the politics of disaffection, the point beyond which the alienated find it difficult to go—not because they may not want to but because they find it hard to conceive what doing so entails? And what allows a liberal society to tolerate discontent and disorder—even when protest becomes illiberal, as sometimes it will? These are the questions the next chapters take up.

4

Alienation and the Idea of America

The idea of America envelops Americans. It is difficult, perhaps particularly for Americans, to appreciate its grip. But we must if we are to see the limits to alienation in this society, if we are to understand better the question of loyalty. On this count the disaffected are the best witnesses. They are convincing witnesses because they are reluctant ones. There is much about American politics that they cannot abide; and they do not hesitate to say so. But there are other things they cannot avoid saying, and still others that they cannot quite bring themselves to say, that underscore the tenacity of the idea of America.

My object is to convey some sense of the limits of what the disaffected can conceive politically. But there is one point to make at the start. If they suffer a foreshortening of political perspective it is not for want of mental acuity. The notion that in politics the extremes are alike, and given alike to oversimplification, is an old one. And we have seen that to be true of the two extremes—the most alienated and the most allegiant. But that does not mean that they are, even comparatively, intellectually impaired or impoverished.

It is tempting, I admit, to write off the disaffected as simply lacking an appreciation of complexity or a tolerance of ambiguity, to see them as prone to thinking in overly simplified, black-and-white terms, to detect in their lack of a balanced judgment of government a familiar sign of an ignorant or intolerant mind. That was my first thought. After all, many aberrations of political belief—prejudice, chauvinism, a lack of commitment to democratic values—spring from an inability to learn the fundamental values of a liberal society.[1]

The disaffected's judgment of government is overly simplified; but is it because they are given to simplistic thinking? Evidently not. We have three tests of cognitive capacities.[2] The first assesses recognition of word meaning. It gives, so to speak, a verbal IQ.[3] We presented respondents with six words, each printed in capital letters on a card, followed by five other words. We then asked them to tell us which of the other words came closest to the meaning of the word in capital letters.

Table 23 shows that those without balance are as verbally aware as those with it—an outcome incompatible with any hypothesis of cognitive simplism. There is nothing to choose between the supportive and the committed in their capacity to get five or more words correct. The test is admittedly crude; yet, even so, the findings should dispel any notion that in speaking of the disaffected—or the committed—we are speaking of the illiterate or ignorant. Intellectual sophistication may not be their mark; but neither is cognitive simplism.

Second, we have measures of political awareness. There is the matter of political interest. If the disaffected—or the committed, since both lack balance—suffer from cognitive simplism, we would expect them to be comparatively indifferent and inattentive to politics. As the table

1. For a recent review of this line of argument and the empirical research—particularly bearing on prejudice—see Harold E. Quinley and Charles Y. Glock, *Anti-Semitism in America* (New York: The Free Press, 1979).

2. A fourth is the findings on education presented in the preceding chapter.

3. For further details see Appendix B.

TABLE 23. COGNITIVE SIMPLISM
(% DOWN – BAS)

	Disaffected (N = 171)	Disenchanted (N = 193)	Middle (N = 154)	Supportive (N = 256)	Committed (N = 226)
Verbal IQ index, number right:					
0	1%	1%	9%	2%	6%
1	4	1	5	1	3
2	5	1	7	4	8
3	10	14	10	8	6
4	13	22	21	16	18
5	31	30	22	40	31
6	37	30	26	29	29
How interested are you in politics and government?					
Very interested	32	23	20	26	26
Fairly interested	42	53	36	42	44
Only a little interested	17	19	24	26	23
Not at all interested	9	6	20	7	8
Political knowledge index: *					
Low	19	39	35	18	42
Middle	52	27	46	47	45
High	29	34	19	35	13

How closely do you follow the news of national events and national problems?					
Very closely	31	28	28	27	25
Pretty closely	46	50	39	47	52
Not too closely	24	21	32	26	23
How often this last week did you watch the *news* broadcasts on television?					
Not at all, or has no TV	18	13	18	12	14
Once or twice	17	17	18	17	12
Three or four times	12	17	13	16	13
Almost every day	17	16	14	13	17
Every day	36	35	37	42	45
How often this last week did you read news stories in the newspapers?					
Not at all, or does not read	18	20	24	14	15
Once or twice	14	11	13	11	12
Three or four times	12	11	5	13	9
Almost every day	13	11	10	7	11
Every day	43	47	47	54	54

*Mailback.

shows, the committed are as interested in politics as the supportive, the disaffected as interested as the disenchanted. More decisive is the matter of knowledge. How much a person says he cares is one thing; how much he knows is another. Our measure of political knowledge assesses primarily whether an individual can recognize discrete bits of knowledge about elementary aspects of the American political process—for example, the proportion of the federal budget devoted to defense or the propensity of blacks to vote for the Republican party. The table indicates the disaffected though not the committed to be as knowledgeable as those who have balance, and reveals no gap in understanding or oversimplification in thought.

A last test is information consumption, that is, the number and regularity of channels of communication a person draws upon. Again those without balance show themselves the equals of those with it. The former are as likely as the latter to report following the news of national events and national problems very closely, watching the news broadcasts on television every day or almost every day and, last, reading news stories in the newspapers every day or almost every day. The disaffected's judgment of government may be oversimplified, but they betray no sign of a generalized tendency to simplism in thought, attention, interest or knowledge.

The disaffected—or the committed—may lack balance, but not in some global or metaphysical sense. It is their judgment of government, not their judgment generally, that is the crux of things. Both the disaffected and the committed are, after all, defined by the one-sidedness of their evaluations of government, by their overreadiness to see it as bad in every respect and good in none, or the other way about. They are given to this way of thinking when it comes to politics—and only to politics.[4]

4. This, of course, is a decisive point of difference with familiar forms of "extremism" turned up in attitude surveys, which are characterized by the

It is not unreasonable to speculate that the lack of a balanced judgment of government is a sign of a weakness of restraint, an impulsiveness in making evaluations if not in taking actions, an inclination to extremity. But if those who lack balance—the committed as well as the disaffected—suffer such an inclination, I suspect it is a selective one. It is the issue of government that excites them, occasions a loss of balance in judgment, inclines them to extremities in evaluation.

Let me say what I mean by such a bias to extremities. A person, if asked, might profess himself to be *very* satisfied with his health. Suppose we were to continue on and inquire how satisfied he was with his car, home, career, personal appearance and the like. We should expect him to reply sometimes that he is *very* satisfied (or dissatisfied) and sometimes that he is *somewhat* satisfied (or dissatisfied). We should be taken aback if he were monotonously to declare that he was very or extremely satisfied with virtually everything. Were he to speak in this fashion, that would surely be an aspect of his thinking, a style of judgment, that we would think worth remarking. Such a habit of mind I shall label "extremity bias."

In talking about politics, those who lack balance should be given to extremes in evaluation, the disaffected pronouncing themselves very dissatisfied, the committed declaring themselves very satisfied. But I do not believe they will show an across-the-board tendency to do this. They should generally sound like others of similar background or circumstances. If their judgments about politics are oversimplified, it is not because they are simple-minded. It may profit us to halt for a moment to listen to the actual words of one of the many we interviewed, when

---

generality of the tendency to oversimplification, dichotomous thinking and the like. See especially Herbert McClosky, "Personality and Attitude Correlates of Foreign Policy Orientation," in James Rosenau, ed., *Domestic Sources of Foreign Policy* (New York: The Free Press, 1967), pp. 51-110.

they were at liberty to speak fully and freely, to hear at first hand contrasting styles of expression. I shall call her Mary. Mary was thirty years old in 1972 and earned between $12,000 and $15,000 as a clinical laboratory technician. She is a college graduate; and she is disaffected. When asked "What things are you satisfied with about America these days, what things do you like about the country?" she replies, "I don't know if I'm particularly satisfied with anything." By "anything," I should emphasize, she means politics; and when she speaks of politics she is eschatological:

The world is going to fall off the edge in the near future. It might very well. I feel cynical about anybody being able to change what is going on. I feel powerless and it is all a big mess. I look at Watergate it is just as if the bag that contained all that stuff burst and the worms are crawling out, and you just get a chance to see it and then somebody will snatch it up and then you will forget about the worms and then it will be the same stuff going on.

Little comment is called for, except perhaps to note that when talking about politics her speech can be hyperbolic. In her apocalyptic tone and scatologic imagery Mary displays an inclination to extremes in evaluation. More instructive is the contrast in tone and style of speech when Mary talks about an issue which is not overtly political. Consider what she says about the standard of living in America:

To me a high standard of living is clean water, clean air, good nourishing food that doesn't have a bunch of pesticides in it and just enough clothes to keep me comfortable. I know myself, I spend a lot of money on buying all kinds of things. I think there are two kinds of materialism—it is wrong to say, but I think it is sort of useless to say that it is bad to be materialistic because to do the work of living, you have to be materialistic in that you need tools to do it, and it is not wrong to have those.

In fact, I think it is wasteful of natural resources to waste tools. I thought about that during the Haight-Ashbury thing when there were all these hippies saying don't worship material things. Like I went to some hippie pads in the Haight-Ashbury, and they would have things, but to show their disdain for them, they would handle them in such a way they got wrecked very quickly. That is just as bad as the people they were condemning for buying a bunch of things and wanting to acquire more things, because they are still wasting raw materials . . . .

As her own words make plain, on this matter Mary has a sense of irony and complexity. She recognizes the importance of technology, despite an aversion to the role it has assumed in the culture. She insists that there can be two kinds of materialism, or more than one type of philistine. Her critique of one critique of materialism is pointed and perceptive. Her judgments are balanced.

The issue is not whether she is insightful, or whether her views are well argued or agreeable. Rather, it is a particular quality of judgment that I wish to call attention to, an awareness that questions are not black and white, a recognition that there is something to be said for "the other side." It is in this sense that her judgment is balanced. Moreover, it would be a serious error to equate having a balanced judgment with taking a middle-of-the-road position. To be balanced is not at all the same thing as being wishy-washy; nor is it a synonym for the empty-headed dialectic of "on the one hand, on the other." Mary has strong convictions about materialism in American life, and her overall stand can scarcely be described as middle of the road. What matters is that her judgments about "materialism" and about politics patently differ in character and quality. Specifically, she is given to extremes in evaluation when she speaks of politics; however, she shows no signs of an extremity bias when she speaks of materialism or other questions outside of politics.

Mary, I believe, illustrates the rule, and not the exception to it. In general, we should expect that those who lack balance in their judgments about government will *not* be marked by a bias to the extremes. Quite the contrary: people who lack balance in their judgments of politics may well possess it in other areas of their life; indeed, they may lack balance at one time and enjoy it at another, usually less frenetic, time.

If my reasoning is sound, we need two measures of extremity bias. One measure should tell us the way a person tends to evaluate political figures or institutions, the other should indicate the way he tends to evaluate nonpolitical ones. We asked many questions about the quality of life. Perhaps it may be worthwhile indicating how extensive and diverse this inquiry was. We asked, among other things, how satisfied the respondents were with the quality of products they buy in the store, the amount of freedom in sexual matters today, the opportunities for racial minorities to get ahead, the move toward complete equality between men and women, the way the United States treats other countries, the nation's efforts to stop pollution of air and water, their family income, the kind of work they do, the amount of time they have for leisure and recreation, the cost of their house or apartment, the kind of people who live in their neighborhood, the place of religion in American life, the way schools educate children for later life and the respect shown for other people's feelings and opinions. And lengthy as this list of examples is, I should emphasize that it is only illustrative, not exhaustive.

There is more than one way to build a measure of extremity bias, but I shall take the most straightforward. For each topic we inquired about, we asked the Mailback respondents to indicate how satisfied (or dissatisfied) they felt by checking a number on a "scale" ranging from one to five. A label accompanied, or "anchored," each number. Thus a one indicated that the respondent was *very* satisfied, a two that he was *somewhat* satisfied and so on. It is worth keeping in mind that the respondent also had the option of checking a box, labeled "undecided," if he couldn't decide how he felt about the topic or if it did not apply to him. To construct an index of extremity bias, I summed the number of times each person placed himself at the extremes, whether he said he was very satisfied or very dissatisfied, first for all the political topics, then for all the remaining ones.

The data bear out my expectations. I performed an analysis of variance on the two measures of extremity bias, one political, the other not. As table 24 shows, those who lack balance in their orientations toward the government are more likely to take the most extreme position in their evaluations, *provided it is some political figure or institution they are evaluating.* But this distortion of judgment is not an across-the-board affair, intruding regardless of the content of the question or the area of life. Those who lack balance—the committed and the disaffected—are neither more nor less likely than those who

TABLE 24. BALANCE AND EXTREMITY BIAS
(MAILBACK)

	Political extremity bias Mean	Nonpolitical extremity bias Mean
Disaffected (N = 31)	36.8	31.
Disenchanted (N = 41)	18.7	25.
Middle (N = 26)	36.6	30.8
Supportive (N = 66)	24.5	26.3
Committed (N = 31)	47.5	30.8

F = 5.493, p≤.05   F = .561, n.s.

possess it to be inclined to extremes in evaluation outside of politics.

It comes down to this: in their evaluations of political matters the disaffected, and the committed, are prone to extremity bias; outside politics, they are just like anyone else, neither more nor less likely to suffer this failing. And to appreciate that those who lack balance in their judgment of government may be virtually indistinguishable, even on close inspection, from others who share in a broad way the same outlook on government is no small point. It does make plain how very hard it is to tell when a citizen has too much enthusiasm for authority, or too little.

But what, we must ask, does disaffection amount to? It is not a pose struck for effect; or it would not impel people into protest, and into a combative style of protest at that. But what are its limits? The disaffected are thoroughly, insistently, stridently alienated—and identified with the idea of America.

A hypothetical example may help. Suppose we were to interview a longtime owner of an Edsel and ask whether he liked his car. He might reply that parts were increasingly difficult to obtain, gas mileage was poor and reliability was uncertain—all in all, that owning an Edsel was a trial. But if we asked outright whether he preferred his Edsel to some comparable alternative, say a new Ford or Chevrolet, without withdrawing one complaint he might well declare his Edsel superior.

As this hypothetical example suggests, there may be a difference between *implicit* and *explicit* comparisons. When investigators have studied alienation, they have asked citizens how they feel about America without explicitly putting an alternative against which they might make their evaluation. They have not asked citizens directly and unambiguously how they feel about the government of this country, *compared with the government of some other country.*

In this study we did ask respondents how the United States compares with most other modern countries. The points of comparison were numerous and various. We touched on a number of areas of life, including education, mobility, minority rights, health care and crime. In addition, we inquired about several manifestly political areas, including freedom of speech and quality of government. For each area of comparison, respondents were asked to check one point on a five-point scale, where every point was explicitly labeled, ranging from "much better" at one pole to "much worse" at the other.

Consider freedom of speech. As we have seen, the disenchanted are patently alienated, even if not as alienated or not alienated in the same way as the disaffected. Yet on freedom of expression the disenchanted hold as high an opinion of the United States as do the supportive (see table 25). Nearly all concur that freedom of speech prospers in the United States, *compared* with most other modern countries. The disaffected may be less enthusiastic, but they are predominantly of the view that matters are somewhat better, even if not much better, here than elsewhere. At a minimum, even the disaffected are free of a disposition to think that other countries are superior when it comes to freedom of speech.

Perhaps a trick in the wording of the question is responsible. If one were argumentative, one might contend that the way we phrased the question so constrained the respondents that they felt that they could not, or should not, pass a negative judgment on the United States. But just to glance at their answers to questions about other areas of life is sufficient to disabuse us of this notion. In a number of areas, substantial proportions, particularly but not exclusively among the alienated, feel that conditions

TABLE 25. EXPLICIT COMPARISON
(% DOWN – MAILBACK)

How do you think the United States compares with most modern countries in these areas of life?	Disaffected (N = 31)	Disenchanted (N = 41)	Middle (N = 26)	Supportive (N = 66)	Committed (N = 31)
Freedom of speech:					
Much better	21%	66%	38%	61%	77%
Somewhat better	57	34	46	33	60
Neither better nor worse	18	0	8	6	3
Somewhat worse	4	0	8	0	3
Much worse	0	0	0	0	0
Opportunity to get ahead:					
Much better	20	39	50	56	87
Somewhat better	56	54	50	33	10
Neither better nor worse	24	7	0	11	3
Somewhat worse	0	0	0	0	0
Much worse	0	0	0	0	0
Personal safety from crime:					
Much better	0	5	17	9	13
Somewhat better	4	23	21	22	27
Neither better nor worse	37	18	25	32	30
Somewhat worse	37	39	29	25	27
Much worse	22	15	8	12	3

Protection of the environment:

Much better	0	5	25	9	19
Somewhat better	15	11	21	27	48
Neither better nor worse	50	54	46	39	16
Somewhat worse	35	30	0	25	13
Much worse	0	0	8	0	3

Quality of education:

Much better	14	30	33	30	36
Somewhat better	21	40	46	24	42
Neither better nor worse	25	50	13	26	7
Somewhat worse	36	13	0	17	16
Much worse	4	3	8	3	0

Rights of minority groups:

Much better	12	29	46	23	56
Somewhat better	27	29	25	36	26
Neither better nor worse	54	42	29	34	15
Somewhat worse	8	0	0	6	4
Much worse	0	0	0	6	0

Health care for everyone:

Much better	0	15	29	12	48
Somewhat better	24	20	17	26	29
Neither better nor worse	24	17	25	31	13
Somewhat worse	36	44	25	28	10
Much worse	16	5	4	3	0

Table 25 (continued)	Disaffected	Disenchanted	Middle	Supportive	Committed
Treatment of the poor:					
Much better	4	13	5	20	35
Somewhat better	11	35	50	33	31
Neither better nor worse	44	25	32	29	17
Somewhat worse	33	23	9	18	17
Much worse	7	5	5	0	0
Quality of government:					
Much better	4	21	35	31	50
Somewhat better	30	32	26	40	33
Neither better nor worse	37	42	35	25	13
Somewhat worse	19	0	4	5	3
Much worse	11	5	0	0	0
Freedom to live as you please:					
Much better	11	35	63	58	57
Somewhat better	26	48	25	29	33
Neither better nor worse	52	18	12	12	7
Somewhat worse	4	0	0	2	0
Much worse	7	0	0	0	3
The American form of government is:					
1. Very close to the worst possible	4	2	0	2	3
2.	14	10	0	0	0
3.	46	39	32	19	10
4.	18	34	32	39	31
5. Very close to the best possible	18	15	36	41	55

here are either somewhat worse, or indeed much worse, than elsewhere. Personal safety from crime, health care for everyone, treatment of the poor, protection of the environment, all are the target of criticism. Quite simply, citizens do not praise their country because they cannot criticize it.

Moreover, when criticism is voiced, it is remarkably muted for those areas of life touching on fundamental aspects, symbolic or institutional, of the political order. Only a handful judge the United States to be in any degree worse as far as the freedom to live as one pleases. Perhaps even more surprisingly, only a similar scattering, even among the alienated, are prepared to say straight out that the rights of minority groups are in any measure worse here than elsewhere.

To be sure, the outlook of the alienated is equivocal, with most of them viewing the United States as neither better nor worse than most other modern countries, at least with respect to these two facets of life. Nonetheless, the outcome seems remarkable on reflection. The issue of minority rights is, to say the least, emotionally charged; for many, especially among the embittered, it has become a symbol of the worst in the American experience. More broadly, we have seen that the disaffected and the disenchanted alike are perfectly capable of railing against the United States. And with this in mind, perhaps it is not unreasonable to characterize the views of the alienated, when confronted with an explicit comparison, as remarkably restrained, if not surprisingly positive.

Then, too, in certain areas of life of singular importance in a democratic society, even the sentiments of the most politically embittered are unambiguously affirmative. One such area is freedom of speech, not an altogether trivial matter for a society pledged to democratic values. Another is the opportunity to get ahead. On both

counts, the disenchanted and the disaffected assert overwhelmingly that things are better here than elsewhere;
indeed, there is not a sole dissenting voice even whisper-
ing that things are better elsewhere than here.
Consider now the question of the quality of government. Surely it is on this point that the alienated should
erupt in criticism. One has only to recall the sentiments
that are the signature of the politically alienated. They
are overwhelmingly of the view that public officials are
insincere, untrustworthy, incompetent, dishonest, unrepresentative and unresponsive; that the government causes
rather than cures many of the country's maladies, that it
cannot be depended on to tell the truth, that it only pre-
tends to care about people's needs. Against this backdrop,
the present finding stands in sharpest contrast: the judgment of the alienated, and the disenchanted particularly,
is favorable. Specifically, slightly in excess of half of the
disenchanted declare that the quality of government is
better in the United States, compared with most other
modern countries. To be sure, a substantial minority of
the disaffected state that the quality of government is in
some degree worse in the United States. But a further
word may place this in perspective.

From one angle, it is as though we had two yardsticks,
or measures, of alienation—the typology of orientations
toward the government and the questions on quality of
government. The adjective checklist, the basis for my typology of alienation and allegiance, is a comparatively
strict measure; the question on the quality of government
is a lenient one. The checklist consists of a large number
of questions, eighteen in all, tapping a variety of facets of
attitudes toward the national government. In contrast,
there is but one question on the quality of government
and, like any one question, it is in several aspects ambiguous. For example, the expression "quality of govern-

ment" may be variously understood. Nor is it clear, for that matter, how much weight to attach to the answer "somewhat worse."

But consider how different the world appears depending on which of these two indices of alienation we look at. If we rely on the strict measure, and implicit comparison, fully thirty-seven percent of the Mailback respondents are politically alienated. Yet if we make use of the lenient measure, but explicit comparison, no more than eight percent are alienated. And at that we are being accommodating, for by alienated we merely mean those who say that the quality of government in the United States, compared with most other modern countries, is *in any degree worse*. If we stiffen the standard and require that to be classified as politically embittered a person must say not only that the quality of government here is worse but that it is much worse—not at all an unreasonable request if our aim is a muscular definition of political alienation— the proportion of alienated plummets to a mere three percent.

What should we make of this? Are there a sizable number, in the Bay Area at least, who in some substantial sense of the word are alienated? Or are there only a bare handful? It very much seems to depend on whether we allow people, in rendering their judgment, to proceed on the basis of implicit comparison—typically the way we do things in research or, for that matter, life—or require them to make an explicit comparison, with the alternatives, standard and focus of comparison unequivocally and unmistakably set out. But perhaps the issue is not so much explicit comparison as the particular comparison. Might the enormous shrinkage in the ranks of the alienated when they are asked to make a direct comparison between here and elsewhere have something to do with our asking them to compare the United States with "most other modern countries"? It is conceivable that people may think exceedingly well of some particular modern country, but far less of some others. Or, even more basically, one may ask what is the decisive comparison. Is it obvious that it must be between the United States and some actual country? Perhaps it should be between the United States and some ideal political order, which may be only imperfectly expressed, if at all, in any existing country?

The last question is an especially interesting one, and worth considering. It would seem important to uncover how harshly, or how generously, Americans evaluate America, if asked to judge what is against what ought to be. Serendipitously, at one point in the Mailback questionnaire we sought an explicit comparison between the actual and ideal (see table 25). "When you think of the way the American form of government works," we asked, "how close does it come to fitting your idea of what the best possible form of government should be? How close is it to the worst possible form of government?"

There seems to be little alternative preference, for Americans at large, even if they are politically embittered. There is at any rate no alternative political order they can see, or conjure up, that any substantial number will commit themselves to. Only twelve percent of the disenchanted, and eighteen percent of the disaffected, choose a response that is in any degree negative. It is not, we should observe, that an inordinate number of the alienated are enthusiastic, although fully half of the disenchanted and a third of the disaffected believe that the American form of government is somewhat or close to the best possible form of government. What is telling is how few, even among the most embittered, are prepared to express a judgment that is in any measure unfavorable—an outcome especially striking, considering that the alienated came upon this question, explicitly asking for their "overall opinion," immediately after firing off the most critical answers to a battery of specific questions about the quality of American government. That is, I believe, one measure of the tenacity of the grip of the idea of America on Americans: they can conceive of no preferable polity, in this world or any other.

The choice we thought we had to make—whether there are a great many alienated or hardly any—is a false choice. It is false *not* in the sense that the figures are somehow a trick of question wording. Rather, people are being called upon to make two different kinds of judgment, depending on whether the comparison is explicit or implicit. An explicit comparison calls upon them for an evaluation of their country *compared with some clearly specified alternative*; their judgment understandably is more likely to be tempered, deliberate, restrained. But to observe that people may make rather different judgments in different situations, depending on whether the comparison is explicit or implicit, is not to say that they mean one of them, and not the other. Both judgments may be valid indicators of their sentiments. But until now we have had to rely on implicit comparisons in the study of alienation, and so have missed seeing the impressive element of "comparative pride," even among the thoroughly cynical.[5]

The Question of Exit

America alone lacks a tradition of emigration. To be sure, since the Revolution and the United Empire Loyal-

5. Roberta Sigel has acutely noted this possibility, underscoring its importance in a discussion of "comparative pride" (the phrase is hers). See Roberta S. Sigel and Marilyn Brookes Hoskin, "Affect for Government and Its Relation to Policy Output among Adolescents," *American Journal of Political Science* 21 (February 1977): 111-134.

ists, there have been flights. But the idea of another promised land, one that might surpass the promise of America, has never taken hold among Americans. Even in the bitter years this study records, few pay lip service to the notion of leaving America and living elsewhere. For most, the prospect of living in another country, whatever they happen to think of this country, is unappealing, even disquieting. For example, we asked respondents how they would feel if they "had to pull up stakes and move to another country." As table 26 shows, by far the overwhelming number are of the opinion that "it would bother [them] a lot." Only among the disaffected was there more than a sprinkling willing to declare that leaving "wouldn't bother [them] very much."

The question of exit may present itself with varying degrees of explicitness, immediacy, severity and irreversibility. Among its guises is a sense of disjunction, of being separate, removed and apart, of not belonging. Such a sentiment of separation may be strategically equivocal: it permits one to express a feeling of rejection, without being bound or expected to act upon it and actually leave America. For this reason, we might expect it to enjoy some currency. Yet the contrary is the case. A sense of belonging suffuses the sentiments of citizens, even if they are alienated. For example, we asked respondents to choose between the following pair of statements:

A. The way this country is going, I often feel that I really don't belong here.
B. Although our country may be facing difficult times, I still feel that it is a worthwhile place and that I really belong here.

Our respondents are unanimous in their sentiment, or nearly so: ninety-seven percent of all expressing their opinion declared that they "really belong here." Even among the disaffected, four in every five rejected the role of outsider, choosing instead to express their sense of belonging, of attachment.

TABLE 26. A QUESTION OF EXIT
(% DOWN – MAILBACK)

	Disaffected (N = 31)	Disenchanted (N = 41)	Middle (N = 26)	Supportive (N = 66)	Committed (N = 31)
If I had to pull up stakes and move to another country:					
It would bother me a lot.	50%	76%	74%	94%	77%
It wouldn't bother me very much.	50	24	26	6	23
The way this country is going, I often feel that I really don't belong here.	19	3	0	0	0
or					
Although our country may be facing difficult times, I still feel that it is a worthwhile place and that I really belong here.	81	97	100	100	100
The people who have dropped out of society and moved to the country have the right idea, and I sometimes feel like joining them.	41	40	0	20	4
or					
People who have dropped out of society may have some real complaints, but I think they're wrong to give up on society so easily.	59	60	100	80	96

"Dropping out" is in some aspects an attenuated version of exit. At the manifest level it is an expression of a sense of separation and disjunction, a feeling of not belonging to or not identifying with the larger society, a stance of spurning the practices and institutions of the official culture. At other than the manifest level, "dropping out" may involve a heightened affinity with certain values of the larger society (for example, "self-realization"), even as it centers on a hostility to other of its values (for example, "achievement"). Moreover, dropping out evokes a life-style which the larger society has publicized in recent years, a way of life that certain segments of the society—in particular, fashionable opinion—have praised and even promoted.

Yet by a lopsided margin people reject this version of exit, at least as we phrased it. We asked them to choose between the following statements:

A. The people who have dropped out of society and moved to the country have the right idea, and I sometimes feel like joining them.

B. People who have dropped out of society may have some real complaints, but I think they're wrong to give up on society so easily.

It is not merely that citizens generally have little sympathy for the notion of dropping out; it could hardly be otherwise, even in the heartland of the counter-culture. What is telling is that even among the disaffected a solid majority lines up against those who have dropped out.

But if we wish to catch a glimpse of the tenacity of the grip of the idea of America on Americans, we should listen to what Americans say, and how they sound, when they speak about leaving America. In the course of the extended interviews we asked whether they felt like outsiders and if they would consider leaving the country. We pressed them to take seriously an idea nearly none had considered seriously. Our purpose, of course, was not to determine the number who had formulated such a plan but to observe the play of ideas, sentiments and symbolic associations which the question of leaving America evokes in Americans. The data, I should add, are neither systematic nor quantitative. Rather, I will attempt to convey by selected illustrations some aspects of the meaning for Americans of leaving, or contemplating leaving, America. Since the disaffected alone pay even lip service to the idea of exit, what they say—and what they do not say—when pressed to air their views in their own words should prove all the more enlightening.

At one level the answer to the question of exit is immediate and straightforward. Only two of the disaffected could bring themselves to say yes, they would leave the country and live in another. And one of them is a ringer. She had lived in Sweden with her mother and family for a number of years, returning to America only to care for her sick father, planning to return to her home in Sweden on his death. She will leave "not because I am trying to move away from this and going to that, but simply because my relatives are there." In short, Americans tend not to want to leave here and live elsewhere, however alienated and embittered they are.

This aversion to leaving America is striking, perhaps particularly since we are speaking not of Americans in general, but of the disaffected in particular. Moreover, the question we put to them was flagrantly hypothetical. "Would you go," we asked, "if you did not have to leave your family and friends?" We virtually invited some of them to say yes, but nearly all of them said no. Yet an exploration of their answers is in order if we are to appreciate the hold of the idea of America on Americans.

The answer is most often immediate and abrupt. "No," one replied, "I have never put any thought into anywhere else." "No," another declared, "it hasn't occurred to me at all to go anywhere else." For both these people, and others like them, the idea of leaving America for a life in another country is literally inconceivable, although both are bitterly critical of American society and politics. In their replies we can see flashes of the power of the idea of America. One person interrupted himself and exploded into speech:

I said a lot of bad things, but I am happy, and I am going to say it again, that I am able to say those things because I couldn't say those things, because I couldn't say them in no other country.

When asked whether he would like to live somewhere else, he answered:

No way, no way. I was in [the Army] for five years and twenty-eight days. And I said when I get back to the good old U.S.A., I don't even want to go on a vacation elsewhere. I am happy right here in Fremont, or in the desert of Arizona—you name it, as long as I can think of living right here in the U.S.

The replies vary in texture, if not in tone. Naturally, some are more elaborate or pungent or thoughtful, and though by virtue of this they are uncommon, they throw a strong light on the immediacy and the tenacity of the ties between self and society. For example, one young woman, when asked whether she would even consider living elsewhere, declared:

I visited Israel for three months and stayed there. And I like to visit, but I don't think I could adjust to living there. The women are in a kind of secondary role, and there's so much work. You have to get up and dress for shopping every day. . . . It's all dry and dirty all the time. I went to a couple more countries on the way back and I don't think I could be able to adjust to another culture, feel completely at home, so that I would feel more like an Algerian than an American. Something like Canada, but Canada seems pretty similar to America. But there's so many things to get used to. I found myself missing foods and speaking English, hearing [people] speak English. Even in England they speak English different. I might want to live some place for a couple of years, a couple of years in different places, but I don't think I'd consider being permanently there.

"Even in England they speak English different." Nowhere else can she imagine herself really feeling at ease and at home, despite her stays abroad. Americans cannot see themselves except as Americans. Even when some, for a moment, can conceive of themselves moving to another country, it is as though they hasten to deny or mock this small disloyalty. So one, on saying he can see himself living elsewhere, tacks on at once the declaration that he can see himself "living within the restrictions of another society only in order to find out about that society." Leaving is conceivable only when it is inconceivable, at least for him: to take up permanent residence in another country would be to undertake a "permanent masquerade."

Others may confront the idea of leaving only if they evade it in the guise of fantasy. For example, one young man can take seriously the notion of quitting America to live elsewhere only if he treats it frivolously. Emigration is acceptable to him only if he thinks of it as a "vacation." And his use of "vacation," like another's use of "masquerade," drives home how one can deny the idea of exit even as one expresses it. When asked if he can think of another area of the country of the world he would prefer, the young man replies:

Only that I would go to a warm area. I should like warm weather with ocean body-surfing—San Diego. I don't know about the weather, but San Diego is half cement, which means that I would at least have to go to Hawaii, Africa, or, I don't know, some coast . . . Mexico.

The imagery of the fabulous may also expose the words as empty. Consider another of the disaffected, poor and poorly educated. She declares that she has thought a lot about leaving the country. She says that she and her boyfriend "would have liked to go to Australia, but didn't have $27,000 to build a boat." What is remarkable is not the extravagance of the imagery, but how alternative countries are seen as variations of and not alternatives to the idea of America. She sees other countries as modifications of here; they may be better in one respect, say, size, and bad or worse in another, say, taxes, but at bottom they are just another version of America. That, at least, is how she speaks of Australia, ostensibly the ideal alternative to America. "But when I start to leave, I start to thinking . . . they have a democracy down there too. It is really not that much different. It's just not as big as we are."

Americans are not uniquely reluctant to imagine themselves leaving their country and living permanently in another. Australians or Russians would by and large be averse to picking up stakes. The reasons are various, and range from ignorance and convenience to chauvinism and principled conviction. But a desire not to leave one's country is one thing; an inability to conceive that one might want to go to another country is quite another. For Americans the idea of America remains the promised land. So it is one thing to criticize it, and quite another to quit it, or even contemplate quitting it. Perhaps, also, what they wish to see helps explain what they cannot see.

Alternative Polities, Alternative Politics

It is the shutting off of alternatives that I should like to discuss. For what marks Americans' sense of America, I think, is as much what it excludes as what it includes. What has fallen by the wayside is a competitive conception of an alternative political order or politics.

The disaffected, at their most eloquent, deliver a jeremiad against the established order.[6] In their denunciation of what is, there are intimations of what should be. For example, which would they favor—our present form of "government by elected representatives," or a government in which there was "personal participation by everyone in all government decisions"? A substantial number of the alienated, and indeed half of the disaffected, favor the wispy vision of personal participation by everyone in all government decisions (see table 27). Even the Constitution, the political instrument and symbolic expression of the American covenant, is not immune to challenge, when a number of the disaffected (though by no means a majority) contend that "this country is having so much trouble dealing with its problems, we should consider making big changes in the Constitution."

In these sentiments, as in others, there is the suggestion that the political order itself should undergo some fundamental change, that it is not just a question of "kicking the rascals out." Indeed, it is more than a suggestion; there is substantial support for the transformation of the American form of government or, at a minimum, a remarkable willingness to approve of such an extraordinary proposal. In the Mailback Survey we asked respondents to choose between the following two statements:

A. Only a very big change in our form of government will allow us to solve this country's problems.
B. We can solve our country's problems without having to make any really big changes in government.

A fifth of the respondents, but the disaffected above all, viewed with favor the idea of transformation.

Of course, what it might mean to make a "very big

6. Bercovitch extracts much from this notion of a jeremiad. See Sacvan Bercovitch, *The American Jeremiad* (Madison: University of Wisconsin Press, 1978).

TABLE 27. MAGNITUDE OF CHANGE
(% DOWN – MAILBACK)

	Disaffected (N = 31)	Disenchanted (N = 41)	Middle (N = 26)	Supportive (N = 66)	Committed (N = 31)
Which would you favor?					
Government by elected representatives.	50%	66%	91%	89%	93%
Personal participation by everyone in all government decisions.	50	34	9	11	7
This country is having so much trouble dealing with its problems, we should consider making big changes in the Constitution.	29	12	27	3	3
Despite some problems, the Constitution works well, and ought to be kept pretty much as it is.	71	88	73	97	97
Only a very big change in our form of government will allow us to solve this country's problems.	58	33	38	9	8
We can solve our country's problems without having to make any really big changes in our form of government.	42	67	63	92	92

Some people believe we need to change our whole system of government in order to solve the problems facing our country, while others feel no real change is necessary. Do you think we:*

Should keep our system of government as it is?	9	23	33	44	59
Need some change in our present system?	70	69	59	55	39
Need a whole new system of government?	21	8	8	1	2

*BAS.

change in our form of government" is open to more than one interpretation, and no doubt some are less ambitious than others. How much support the idea of large-scale change enjoys depends mightily on question wording. For example, we put to respondents the following preamble and question:

Some people believe we need to change our whole system of government in order to solve the problems facing our country, while others feel no real change is necessary. Do you think we need a whole new system of government, some change in our present system, or should we keep our system of government pretty much as it is?

When the question is phrased this way (and an interviewer is present), the level of support for transformations drops sharply: only seven percent were prepared to say that we need a whole new system of government.

How many support the notion of a fundamental change in the form of government? One would like exact answers, but perhaps a matter of higher priority is determining what people have in mind when they call for a "whole new system of government," if indeed they have anything much in mind.

To obtain some sense of what demands for fundamental change might mean, we asked all who called for any measure of change what exactly they had in mind. What kind of change in our system of government, we inquired, were they thinking of? We shall focus on those among the disaffected who called for change in our system of government (rather than diluting the analysis by mixing in all favoring any degree of change, whether they are alienated or not) in order that we may see the boundaries of the idea of fundamental change in America.

A last preliminary. People were at liberty to give more than one answer. Indeed, up to three replies were taken down. We enjoy, then, several options in the analysis of their answers. We might take seriously the order of their replies, and attach more weight to the one that was, so to speak, on the tip of their tongues and less to one that was, as it were, last to mind. But this demands an excessively credulous acceptance of the vagaries of speech. The fairest procedure is to take note of all that was said. Then, too, the fairest procedure happens to afford the stiffest test.

Some organization, of course, had to be imposed on the welter of remarks people voiced. To that end we devised a number of categories and, within each of them, attempted to sift the comments into finer categories yet. Table 28 shows the proportion of all the comments of the disaffected, the disenchanted and so on which fall into the various broad categories.

What do the disaffected who declare that we need a whole new system of government have in mind? When asked to explain, what they most often call for is not a transformation of the system of government at all, but rather a modification of a *specific government policy*. This is not to stigmatize such remarks as inconsequential. People may raise weighty issues—for example, health, education, housing and welfare. Yet two points should be made. First, the readiness with which the disaffected turn to specific issues should alert us to the possibility that they have failed to form a rival conception of politics. Second, if we take a closer look at the particular issues they mention, taking advantage of distinctions within the categories shown in table 28, two stand out: taxes and crime control. The disaffected, it would appear, scarcely focus their attention on revolutionary issues. Their concerns are much like everyone else's—not in every detail, to be sure, but in the main and most salient features.

The disaffected do appeal for change in governmental institutions very nearly as often as they make some remark about a specific governmental policy; and a call for

TABLE 28. WHAT WHOLESALE CHANGE MEANS
(BAS)

Mentions	Disaffected (N = 145)	Disenchanted (N = 136)	Middle (N = 84)	Supportive (N = 127)	Committed (N = 78)
Change government institutions	48%	52%	29%	58%	56%
Change kinds of people in politics	37	29	44	34	22
Change level of popular participation	15	11	8	16	10
Reduce power of (or attention given to) certain social groups	14	15	13	8	6
Increase power of (or fairness for) certain social groups	16	12	14	4	4
Changes phrased in terms of needed ideological shifts	13	6	5	7	6
Change societal values	11	11	4	7	20
Change specific government policies	69	68	78	65	76
Nonspecific references to changes in the system as a whole	26	23	18	23	20
Residual	1	2	2	3	2

Note: We recorded up to three responses; this table is based on all responses that were recorded.

institutional change has an undeniably more solid ring to it, at least at first hearing. But, then, the fact that such comments are just as likely to be heard among the disenchanted, the supportive or the committed, for that matter, cautions against extravagance in interpretation. What more exactly do the disaffected have in mind by such changes? Most often they wish to alter in some manner the nature, power or functioning of the presidency, the Congress or the courts. (The three, incidentally, receive about equal shares of the critical reviews among the disaffected.) Again, the disenchanted and the rest also talk much the same way, about much the same thing. But my object is not to dismiss what the disaffected have to say as shallow or superficial. All that I wish to remark is that we cannot read into these remarks about the executive and the like any outline of an alternative political order, organized in some radically different way.

The disaffected voice many criticisms. In particular, a number of them criticize the electoral process in general, or call for some unspecified reform of the electoral process; or find fault with the present means of electing a president (for example, attacks on presidential primaries) or the system of campaigning more generally (for example, the ignoring of issues or the undue influence of rich contributors). The question is not whether such criticisms are "merely" reformist or "genuinely" radical; with the information at hand we have no way to tell, even if we could agree on what these terms meant. But the point remains that these are criticisms of the present system, not proposals for an alternative one.

That is an impression reinforced by a look at the third most commonly heard comment: change the kinds of people in politics. "Get new people in politics." That scarcely sounds like the slogan of the revolutionary vanguard. To be sure, a wholesale change of the people in politics could amount to a substantial change. Yet it does seem to miss much of the point if one is bent on the transformation of the political order itself. For a change in personnel, even a sweeping one, is not the same as a change in the political system; or more precisely, perhaps, the two alternatives are likely to be confused by those who have not been able to formulate a competitive conception of a political order.

It is, of course, conceivable that the appeal for this sort of change might amount to something substantial nonetheless. Perhaps it is an expression in shorthand, so to speak, one that has come to symbolize more fundamental forms of change in the minds of Americans. For example, when they call for "new kinds of people" in politics, might they be thinking of people committed to a certain point of view, or identified with the disadvantaged, or pledged to a new form of politics? It is arguable that their minds are occupied with such larger ideas; but after closer examination of their remarks, it seems implausible. More often than not, those calling for new kinds of people in politics have no clear idea at all about the kind of people they want (apart from the occasional call for more blacks) beyond their being in some unspecified way "different."

In what way might they be different? We can catch a glimpse of what the disaffected have in mind by listening to what they dislike about those now in politics in the course of explaining why we need new people to replace them. New politicians are needed, they feel, because the current ones are untrustworthy and insincere, or unresponsive and indifferent, or too old and out of touch. Hackneyed or not, these criticisms draw on a certain naïve moralism, a dissatisfaction with individuals on the grounds of flaws of individual character, as though the challenge were merely to replace a dishonest man with an honest one. Indeed, for more than a few it turns out they are not even bent on turning many out of office; they only want to replace one—for example, Nixon or Reagan. However one looks at it, the appeal for "new people" in politics does not add up to, or even vaguely suggest, a call for far-reaching and fundamental changes in our system of government.

To be sure, a substantial part of what the disaffected had to say was directed at a larger target: changes in the political system as a whole. But it is precisely when they talk of change on this scale that we can see how hollow and vague the notion of fundamental change is—even in the minds of the most politically embittered. Thus most remarks about changes in the system as a whole had to be categorized as "nonspecific." The most one could make out about nearly one in every two such remarks was an expression of the need for major change. What such a change might consist of was so vaporous as to defy detection. And when we can get hold of what they have in mind in calling for changes in the political system as a whole, what they say is jarring. The principal themes, in order of frequency, are: the government's waste and inefficiency, its size, its power; and, perversely, a number of remarks suggest that the system as a whole is indeed working, and in need of only small changes. These remarks hardly smack of a revolutionary design or, perhaps more to the point, an alternative polity or politics.

In fairness, there are calls for a change in the system as a whole, views that are definite and programmatic, phrasing the appeal for change in terms of needed ideological shifts. But it is the number of such remarks, the paucity of them, which is the very first thing one must acknowledge. Of all the replies the disaffected made when asked to explain what they had in mind saying that a whole new system of government was needed, only twenty, in all, are in ideological terms, of whatever character. Of these, a grand total of two call for socialism, while ten appeal for less of a capitalist and more of a socialist society. There is no alternative ideology, no alternative polity, excepting only a lonely voice. Consider one last example. One might think that those who phrase an answer in terms of societal values when asked to explain what they have in mind stand a fair chance of having formed at least a recognizable impression of a political society differing in some fundamental respect from the American model. Closer examination, however, reveals that we are speaking of only a handful of scattered references to a variety of well-publicized complaints, none of which bespeaks a repudiation of the core values of the larger society. For example, social responsibility is the theme most often voiced by the disaffected, that is, the need for people to do their part and fulfill their obligations. Or they talk of the problem of personal isolation and loneliness, that is, the lack of personal closeness, the importance of knowing your neighbors, the need for brotherhood and helping one's fellow man. My point is not that such concerns are superficial or uninstructive, though no doubt they often amount to no more than the mindless repetition of tired clichés. But what matters more is that such expressions are, so to speak, clichés of *this* culture; at a minimum, they do not signify allegiance to, or even any special awareness of, an alternative conception of the political order.

A Final Remark

Some, I grant, may now draw the conclusion that political alienation amounts to something close to pouting, that it does not involve a state of mind sufficiently serious or definite to concern a student of politics. Such a view strikes me as judgmental, excessively so, but it is not on that score I would object to it. One can dismiss the cynicism of the disaffected as not heartfelt or their acts of protest as self-flattery—and not always be wrong. But I find a more straightforward and simpler view of things persuasive: the disaffected are politically suspicious, resentful, disillusioned; given the right chance, they will translate their feelings into actions, and sometimes violent ones at that. And the point I have meant to make is this: one can be alienated, genuinely so, and yet identify with the political order—as the disaffected do.

This is, at bottom, an argument of American exceptionalism. But Americans are surely not unique in the strength of their patriotism. An Englishman or a Russian can be just as reluctant to quit his country. And some part of this sense of American distinctiveness may prove to be no more than ethnocentrism.[7] Without evidence from other countries, one can only speculate. Yet I am persuaded that the political tradition is more hemmed in here than elsewhere. Time has witnessed the eclipse of alternative conceptions of a political order in America. Such alternative conceptions are no longer, to borrow William James's phrase, live hypotheses, except in small folds of the culture. The American at large, even if uncommonly active and politically articulate, does not entertain the notion that some other form of political order is preferable, even if he is bitterly unhappy with the present one. Arguments over government, including its transformation, take place within the American experience, not outside it.

7. Kavanagh warns of this pitfall. See Dennis Kavanagh, "Allegiance Among English Children: A Dissent," *British Journal of Political Science* 2 (January 1972): 127-130.

5

Disorder and the Democratic Idea

Some dismiss as empty rhetoric the political cynicism that many Americans now express; I do not. But it is difficult to avoid exaggeration, to refrain from depreciating the importance of the change in public attitudes that has taken place since the 1960s—or inflating it. And that is partly because much depends on whether citizens' judgment of government is balanced. The measures of attitudes toward the political order now in common use may tell us if Americans trust government less, or believe it is more wasteful, than they used to. But whether any change is salutary or alarming depends not just on the number of citizens who have become alienated; how many of them have a balanced judgment also matters. A jump in cynical remarks about politicians may signify the emergence of a healthy skepticism. Or it may denote embitterment, a one-sidedness and inclination to extremes that propels some into an adversary politics.

So, too, a restoration of trust in government may bespeak measured judgment or excess of faith. This, of course, is an example of something that we have learned that we already knew. Who ever argued that loyalty should be blind? But then, who could tell when it was? Now we can identify, at least approximately, who is overready to approve and who is not. The method I have hit upon is surely not the only one and it is a crude one. People do not either have or not have a balanced judgment, even about government. Balance is a matter of degree, but as a practical matter the best that I could do was to treat it as a dichotomous variable, as something one either has or does not have.

Even so, the importance of seeing who lacks balance— of observing how a lack of perspective may actually express itself and what it may lead to—is plain. Some findings may be surprising. Who would have expected the numbers of the committed to be so large—more than a fifth, in fact—remembering when and where this study was conducted? And everything suggests that their numbers are substantially larger in the country as a whole. But whether something is or is not surprising is beside the point. The basic idea of this study is surely not new, although the attempt to examine it systematically is. And one advantage of trying to make explicit an idea that we always knew is that it makes clearer what, in fact, we don't know. Who can say whether the ranks of the committed, those hard-core believers, shrank after Watergate? Now we can and should.

This study was done under the looming shadow of Watergate; the sample was drawn from the San Francisco Bay Area. An uncommon time, an uncommon place. Add to this a new measurement procedure, a complex study design. One warning should suffice: there is uncertainty as to how dependable and generalizable are the findings of this study. I know of no reliable way to estimate—compared with similar studies—how serious a problem this is.[1]

But what might one honestly be uncertain of? Surely

---

1. The issues are complex; consider the question of generalizability. There is a tendency to deprecate regional samples in favor of national ones, even when the latter are demonstrably less efficient for the problem being investigated. As here: the customary national cross-sectional design would have included too few who had participated in any form of protest to permit systematic analysis. As biases go, the preference for national samples is not unreasonable.

those who think the government is bad in every respect and good in none—or the other way about—are an odd lot?[2] And yet, who cannot be coaxed into acknowledging that nothing is perfect—including the government? What is telling is not a person's ability, if pressed, to admit this homily—in fact, the supportive and the committed are indistinguishable, or nearly so, when both are forced to choose between praising the government and criticizing it. Rather, what counts is a person's readiness to recognize this otherwise obvious point—without benefit of a reward or a reminder.

And a balanced judgment involves more than the ability to cope with a question about government. It is an indication of a certain temper of mind. As is its absence. Those who lack balance—the committed and the disaffected—share a way of thinking about politics, resembling each other in this despite their holding nearly diametrically opposite positions on the merits of the national government, not to mention their differing radically in political conviction and social circumstances. So they are given to a certain uniformity of view. Asked about the rights of government and the duties of citizens, the committed are champions of authority. They are, overwhelmingly, of the view that government has the right to make citizens pay taxes for programs they disapprove of; to make someone obey a law that goes against his conscience; to force citizens to obey a law that they dislike strongly; to require citizens to show respect for the American flag; to require children to attend school even if their parents don't want them to; to require all able-bodied citizens to help during a national emergency, like a flood or an earthquake; to require citizens to serve the country

2. This may be an example of the danger of the obvious. Very much to the point are the findings that in many important respects those who lack balance are not an odd lot at all.

in some way during a war they disapprove of.[3] Some of these propositions command support across the board, the obligation to help in an emergency being the best example. But only the committed back all of them, and always by a lopsided margin.

The disaffected show a similar uniformity—lining up on the opposite side of the fence from the committed but lining up all the same. The disaffected alone are predominantly of the view that a citizen should not have to underwrite programs he disapproves of; or be required by government to show respect for the American flag; or be obliged to serve in the armed forces; or obey a law that goes against his conscience—even after Congress and the courts have confirmed the validity of the law. The disaffected are not mindless in this opposition to authority, any more than the committed are mindless in their support for it. Both are capable of making exceptions—the committed are opposed to mandatory voting, for instance, and the disaffected favor compulsory schooling. But the views of both are distinguished by a rather single-minded consistency: both stamp their broad orientations toward government on their reactions to specific questions on the rights it is entitled to exercise, on the duties a citizen is obliged to perform. Neither is much impressed or deterred by particulars. Those who lack balance can be counted on to be predominantly of one mind—the committed for, the disaffected against—excepting only when common sense clearly commands otherwise.

In contrast, those with a balanced judgment of government show a certain flexibility. They may side against the government even though they are allegiant, or with it even though they are alienated: their reactions very much depend not just on the broad issue but on the different

3. The data on government rights, drawn from the Mailback, are not shown.

ways it may be formulated. So a majority of the disenchanted oppose the idea that the government has a right to make someone obey a law that goes against his conscience, and support the idea that it may force citizens to obey a law that they dislike strongly. This may give an impression of inconsistency to those who cannot see substantial differences in specific phrasings of a broad principle. But as the disenchanted's judgment of government is differentiated, so their evaluation of its claims is discriminating. The supportive give evidence of a similar attentiveness. They oppose a draft in peacetime and solidly back one during a war. To be sure, a majority of the supportive back much the same claims that the committed do—but not by the same unvaryingly one-sided margin. Asked what a government is entitled to require, and a citizen obliged to do, those with balance show a thoughtfulness those without do not.

This may have a familiar sound to it, one more report that opposites are alike, in politics at least; one more variation on the adage that people who take extreme stands tend to have a closed mind, it being better, presumably, to keep an open one. To a degree; but there are some aspects of this obvious finding which are, in fact, not obvious at all. The disaffected are, of all, the best educated, the committed the worst. Despite this, the two show a comparable coarseness in their thinking about politics. Moreover, what we should admire in a citizen is rather less clear than what we should criticize. That we should not celebrate a closed mind is obvious enough. But should we prize an open one, one which is flexible in just the way that I have illustrated? Is the good citizen really the one who makes up his mind about the question of obligation, issue by issue? Is there much to recommend—except under the most extraordinary circumstances—the willingness of a citizen to weigh his duties against his rights? And this especially if in the process he is careful, disinterested, judicious—what is admirable as a hypothesis only cloaks what would be ridiculous as an everyday practice. Something can be said for constancy. What is there to recommend that citizens look on the claims of government as if each of these should be subject to their scrutiny, as opposed to that of Congress, the courts, all the institutions of representative democracy? There is, after all, a question of loyalty.

There is no proof positive that balanced judgment is what makes a difference between the supportive and the committed or between the disenchanted and the disaffected. There is certainly no direct evidence of there being two dimensions to attitudes toward authority, one reflecting how a person feels toward government (favorably or not), the other how he thinks about it (in a balanced way or not). It may only be that the committed are so very much more positive in their attitudes toward government than the supportive. Or the disaffected so very much more negative than the disenchanted.

There seems to me no decisive way to rule out this interpretation; nor a compelling reason to attempt to. The point to keep uppermost, I believe, is simple enough: the supportive are allegiant, the disenchanted are alienated. The one may not be as enthusiastic as the committed, the other as embittered as the disaffected. There are differences of degree, but they are, by and large, modest ones. And this is no artifact of definition. The disenchanted could have turned out to pay just lip service to the denunciations of the disaffected. Or the supportive could have turned out to be less tenacious or thoroughgoing than the committed in the degree to which they identified with the political order. Then this study's findings would have testified to the importance of intensity, not balance. But what is telling is the similarity between the supportive and the disenchanted. And it is the more impressive in the face of the similarities between the former and the committed and the latter and the disaffected in broad orientation toward government. Whether a person's judgment is balanced, it seems, makes a world of difference. Thus those who are overready to approve of government are overready to yield to it. Pressed to choose, they showed themselves to support tighter controls at the expense of more freedom; to believe that without strong laws most people would behave like animals rather than behave decently; to favor an expansive definition of the rights of government and the duties of citizens. The committed were also more prepared to tolerate a narrowing of civil liberties and civil rights in an effort to improve morals or to fight crime; to believe "my country, right or wrong"; to agree that government may bend or even break the law to "do its job."

Commitment, I think, is different from familiar forms of right-wing extremism. Intolerance on the right, bigotry, superpatriotism take root among the poorly informed, the poorly off and, above all, the poorly educated. The committed were less well educated than the supportive (though not so, it might be remembered, among the young). But they were not socially marginal. Nor were they psychologically crippled.

There are, of course, many varieties of political extremism. Some give themselves away: the sentiments they involve are archaic—old-fashioned isolationism, for example—or they are ostentatiously at odds with official values of the political culture—Maoism, for instance. Commitment is different. There is nothing socially undesirable or even curious about the committed's view of government—except on reflection. What, after all, did the committed do? They may have said that five adjectives—out of a total of eighteen they listened to—were a good description of the government. All five were in some degree favorable, to be sure, but there is no evidence that they—or the interviewer—noticed this. And, strictly speaking, the committed did not assert that the government is free of all faults. Their reaction to an unfavorable adjective was silence: they neither agreed nor disagreed.

What people do not say can be a sign of what they think; but it is usually not an obvious one. Force the committed and the supportive to respond and they would sound alike. The freedom not to react—without this being construed as a sign of either ignorance or disagreement—is critical. Adjective checklists offer this freedom, more conventional question formats do not. Which is both fortunate and not. I chose the checklist out of curiosity; it has been frequently employed by psychologists but only rarely by political scientists. And only after being struck by the notion that there may be two varieties of allegiance did I try to take advantage of this format. In this sense the idea came before the measure, not the other way about. But the very reason that I included a checklist in the first place—its unfamiliarity because of the infrequency of its use in assessing political attitudes—may preclude others, who turn to comparable data gathered in this critical period, from confirming findings that I have reported.

But no study of public opinion is short of drawbacks, among them the difficulty of saying when public opinion will matter. One can guess that some points of view are likely to be politically less important than the number espousing them might suggest because they are self-defeating. Prejudice, for example, tends to spring from ignorance and apathy. It muzzles itself politically to the degree that bigots are inattentive or apathetic.

Many forms of political extremism tend to work against themselves in this way. But not commitment. The committed were as politically attentive as the supportive: they were as interested in news at the national level, followed television or read news stories in the papers as regularly, were as interested in government. The committed were less likely to write to government officials or sign a petition; but they were as likely to vote in a presidential primary or work for a political party or candidate. The committed were less well educated than the supportive and were poorer, too—but only among those who were older, not among those who were thirty-five or younger. Moreover, we know there is no systematic connection between a lack of education and the absence of a balanced judgment. For the disaffected were remarkably well educated. And their evaluation of government was as one-sided as that of the committed.

It is judgment of government, I should emphasize, and not judgment in general which is of interest. It was not politics as usual when this study was conducted. Many citizens felt strongly about what was going on—the war, the antiwar demonstrations, Nixon, Johnson. And about government itself. Some were critical; some were defensive; many were upset. What citizens thought of government was a live issue. The committed and the disaffected were prone to extremity bias in evaluating politics—the immediate focus of contention—but not the quality of life, whatever its larger relevance to specific issues in dispute.

Moreover, they were sometimes capable of a more balanced judgment of government itself. The disaffected gave the impression of harboring a more favorable view of American politics when we brought more pressure to bear upon them to deliberate, to consider the matter more exactly, to contemplate the difference between this country and another—that is, when we asked them to make an explicit comparison rather than rely on the implicit one researchers routinely solicit and respondents reflexively proffer. And when they were more deliberate, there was a suggestion of a more thoughtful reply, as indicated partly by their capacity to differentiate various areas of life, giving America comparatively poor marks in some of them—crime, for one—and rather good grades in others, including freedom of speech and the quality of the government.

It would be mischievous to suggest that because the disaffected did not especially like somewhere else they did not really dislike things here. Yet their repudiation plainly had limits. The disaffected were critical, resentful, cynical, embittered. Because they were, their reluctance to quit America, or to contemplate the idea of leaving it, is the more impressive. The evidence is difficult to weigh. There were, after all, Americans who left the country to protest the war or avoid the army. Yet America has no tradition of emigration. And rereading the depth interviews, in which we did our best to encourage or prod respondents to tell us how they actually felt, I am struck again by the extent to which the idea of America envelops Americans: even among the disaffected who openly called for a change in the system of government there was no intelligible trace of an alternative political vocabulary, of an alternative political order.

Yet the disaffected and the disenchanted did deliver philippics; they also protested.

Political protest comes in all sizes. We looked into four—taking part in a boycott, a peaceful demonstration, a sit-in, a demonstration that turned violent. It was, I think, remarkable how many of our respondents had done at least one of these. No doubt, some said they had when they hadn't; and others construed as protest an act—not buying a nonunion head of lettuce, for instance —which some might not. But against the backdrop of earlier studies of citizen participation, there was an impression of involvement, of citizens actually doing something.

It would be facile to take this bustling about as evidence of all-out commitment. But a substantial number were plainly capable of doing a good deal besides voting, when aroused. More fundamentally, it bears repeating that turning to unconventional forms of involvement, such as protest, was no indication that conventional forms of participation, such as voting, were unacceptable. Then, too, it seems that we should not speak simply of protest, as though its different forms—or at any rate the four we explored—really were aspects of the same phenomenon, differing in degree perhaps, but not in kind. This view is not inconsistent with the analysis of dimensionality, particularly the factor analysis, of the Bay Area Survey. But it is not the only view. One can draw a line, I think, between at least two types of protest. And the empirical findings suggest that this distinction between advocacy and adversary protest is not merely conceivable; it may be profitable.

Advocacy protest enjoyed a broad appeal; it drew substantially, though not evenly, on diverse strata within the community. And that holds for political outlook as well as social circumstances. In contrast, adversary protest had a narrow constituency: the demiclass of the young and well educated, who attended or lived near a university. But the instructive point is this: distinguishing between these two kinds of protest allowed us to see a politically telling distinction between two kinds of alienation. The disenchanted were discontent and, understandably, were more likely than the allegiant to engage in some act of protest. But they were not only less likely to take part in adversary protest than the disaffected; they were no more likely to have done so than the supportive. One can distinguish two kinds of alienation. And it is a distinction that makes a difference, not just in what people say but in what they do. What do these various findings add up to, put most briefly? Two things, I suspect. First, we may have underestimated what citizens are capable of, if they should find themselves in the circumstances of the late 1960s and early 1970s, in terms of both the quality of the judgment they render and the range of action they may explore in a spirit compatible with a democratic politics. Second, we may have overestimated the threat posed by political alienation not because the changes in public attitudes toward political institutions which have excited comment are superficial or merely expressive, but because they may to a very considerable degree reflect a temper of mind congenial to a pluralist society. The first point strikes me as a matter of personal judgment, the second as more consequential; it bears exploring.

One can find among the allegiant or alienated who have balance an awareness of the pitfalls of democratic politics: they are in this respect tough-minded. The classic expression of tough-mindedness about politics—and democratic theory—is *The Federalist*.

Countries are vain, ambitious and aggressive, the *Federalist* contends, because men are vain, ambitious and aggressive. It was the most celebrated of statesmen, Pericles, who launched the Peloponnesian wars, which in the end consumed Athens itself. And he ignited the conflagration not for some lofty public purpose but for two more personal reasons: to quiet Aspasia, a prostitute, who was egging him on to prove his manhood, and to divert attention from charges against him, among them an accusation that he was spending public monies to boost his personal popularity.[4] The "ambitious Cardinal," Wol-

---

4. *The Federalist*, ed. Jacob E. Cooke (Middletown, Conn.: Wesleyan University Press, 1961; also paperbound, Cleveland: Meridian Books, 1961), p. 29; all subsequent references are to this edition.

sey, goaded his king, Henry VIII, to undertake a folly of
a war with France, not to benefit England or his king, but
to place in his own hands the papal triple crown.[5]

The rule of the many, the *Federalist* insists, is no safer
or wiser than the tyranny of the few. Republics have
proven themselves puppets of personal passions as often
as monarchies. And how could it be otherwise? "Are not
the former administered by *men* as well as the latter?"[6]

Because the political is unavoidably personal, it is nec-
essarily fallible. Men can reason many matters out, together as well as alone; they can discover things that belie
as well as things that confirm the senses.[7] But in "the
sciences of morals and politics," duty and desire come
together, and the virtues of "caution and investigation"
may degenerate into the vices of "obstinacy, perverseness
or disingenuity."[8]

To judge by *Federalist* imagery, the civic life is not
redemptive nor even educative, as Mill and many in the
liberal tradition would have us believe.[9] It is probative, at
best. The coincidence of private advantage and public
good is imperfect, and it is always so because it is neces-
sarily so. In a republic, those raised to high office may
enjoy a superior character as well as a superior reputation. But their vocation exposes them to corruption, while
their circumstances render them susceptible to temptation. "In republics, persons elevated from the mass of the
community, by the suffrages of their fellow-citizens, to
stations of great pre-eminence and power, may find com-
pensations for betraying their trust, which to any but
minds animated and guided by superior virtue, may appear to exceed the proportion of interest they have in the

5. Ibid., p. 30.

6. Ibid., p. 32.   7. Ibid., p. 194.   8. Ibid., p. 195.

9. Carole Pateman, *Participation and Democratic Theory* (Cambridge:
Cambridge University Press, 1970).

common stock, and to over-balance the obligations of duty."[10]

The problem of corruption arises, but not principally because men are corrupt. Some are. But even if all the bad were excluded from politics and only the good were admitted to it, some would turn bad under the pressures of civic life. And to understand these pressures is to understand that some would turn bad for good reasons as well as base.

Consider the zeal which participation in public affairs may arouse. Involvement in the public business tends to arouse men's feelings, to heighten a sense of urgency and, when decisions are made collectively rather than individually, to emphasize immediate interests and momentary advantage at the expense of a larger sense of the public interest and common responsibility. Public bodies of men, compared with the same individuals deliberating privately, show less "rectitude" and "disinterestedness," more impetuousness, greater susceptibility to passion and lower regard for reputation—all understandable, according to the *Federalist*, since "the infamy of a bad action is to be divided among a number [of people, as opposed to when] it is to fall singly upon one." Civic men will rush into "improprieties and excesses, for which they would blush in a private capacity."[11]

The civic life puts men to the test when, and because, they accept its responsibilities. Men frequently will differ over what is proper and prudent. But differences which in private life they might resolve or even ignore become for them in public life the source of principled intransigence. The *Federalist* insists on a cruelty of democratic politics when it contends that a special bitterness arises for a losing advocate not because the decision went against

10. *The Federalist*, p. 142.   11. Ibid., p. 96.

him, but because he had a hand in it in the first place. In Hamilton's words:

...if they have been consulted and have happened to disapprove, opposition then becomes in their estimation an indispensable duty of self-love. They seem to think themselves bound in honor, and by all the motives of personal infallibility to defeat the success of what has been resolved upon, contrary to their sentiments. Men of upright, benevolent tempers have too many opportunities of remarking with horror, to what desperate lengths this disposition is sometimes carried, and how often the great interests of society are sacrificed to the vanity, to the conceit and to the obstinacy of individuals, who have credit enough to make their passions and their caprices interesting to mankind.[12]

The *Federalist*'s moral temper is unsparing. Let me begin by remarking what this sensibility is not. It is not, above all, romantic. It insistently rejects any notion that political life turns around a competitive struggle between virtue and vice. Man's world is imperfect. "The purest of human blessings must always have a portion of alloy in them." Good can never be absolute, though evil may threaten to be. "The choice must always be made, if not of the lesser evil, at least of the Greater, not the Perfect good."[13]

One must guard against the good, in politics at least. Seeking it too zealously can excite the imagination into conjuring up "an endless train of possible dangers; and by indulging an excess of jealousy and timidity, we may bring ourselves to a state of absolute scepticism and ir-resolution."[14] The quest for certainty paralyzes all, and so jeopardizes all. Neither risk nor imperfection can be banished. It is "the extreme of imprudence to prolong the precarious state of our national affairs, and to expose the

12. Ibid., p. 475.   13. Ibid., p. 269.   14. Ibid., p. 197.

union to the jeopardy of successive experiments, in the chimerical pursuit of a perfect plan."[15] If prudence is the mood of the *Federalist*, it is a prudence set apart by ambitiousness, audacity, even defiance. So Hamilton brushes aside appeals for delay, with the uncompromising declaration: "I never expect to see a perfect work from imperfect man."[16] That is an extraordinary remark to make, not least for its austerity. The *Federalist*'s view of politics is singular. But a reading of it can alert one to the importance of balance. More broadly, it can remind one that a certain capacity for disillusion—for disorder even—has been a recurrent and prominent feature of the American experience.[17] The American government may enjoy more trust than many but it has not been saved all moments of stress; it has more than once provoked or suffered public cynicism and opposition. My thesis: alienation contributes to the stability and, quite possibly, the vitality of democratic politics by virtue of its *absorption* into the central culture, elite as well as mass, in the form of *diffuse norms*, depending on the *responsiveness* of institutions and the *exhaustiveness* of culture. Let me comment in order on these.

Absorption

The number who think that government officials care more about their own interests than those of the public varies from one country to another, from one time to another. The number who are alienated, and the intensity of their disaffection, obviously matter. But what may

15. Ibid., pp. 590-591.   16. Ibid., p. 591.
17. On this point it is useful to recall Dahl's observation that there has been a serious outbreak of political disorder about once every political generation in the United States. See, for example, Robert A. Dahl, *Pluralist Democracy in the United States* (Chicago: Rand McNally, 1967), pp. 283-286.

matter more is whether this cynicism, this antipolitical view of politics, is absorbed into the mainstream of the political culture itself. For in a democratic politics elites count, too.[18]

From the outset political cynicism in America was directed against political elites by political elites. Less than half a generation after the establishment of the Constitution, those who held power in the Washington community thought of politics as a "species of mania."[19] There were few in a community of people in politics who could be trusted precisely because they were in politics. To be part of a political community was to be a part of a group where no member could count wholly on any other—except to take advantage. Whatever others said they believed, how could one tell what they actually thought or what they were likely to do? There might be profit in politics but there was little honor—and therefore little trust, privacy or fellowship.[20]

But the pursuit of interest is one thing, the ambition for power another. Running through the life of the Washington community was a ceaseless striving to raise oneself high by bringing others low. Wielding power is divisive, seeking it devouring. So at the very inception of the Washington community there was a wedding of the images of power and politics. From the outset there was a widespread wariness of politics, a pervasive suspicion and skepticism of the central institutions of governance, and a deep-seated ambivalence toward the men in public office.

A diffuse cynicism about politics permeated the opinions of those at the center of the society; leaders looked

18. Lacking data, my argument is only speculative; yet I feel I should speculate if only to make clearer my argument. This part of it follows closely Young's singular study, *The Washington Community*. See James Sterling Young, *The Washington Community 1800-1828* (New York: Harcourt, Brace and World, 1966).

19. Young, *Community*, p. 51.   20. Ibid., p. 52.

on other leaders just as followers did. As Young has remarked:

It appears, then, that what the politicians in government pro-
jected upon themselves was essentially the outsiders' image—
the cultural stereotypes—of politicians in power. It appears, in
other words, that we confront the community of power-holders
who shared, to a significant degree, the anti-power outlook in
the values of their culture.[21]

To the degree that the elites shared with citizens at large
this anti-power and anti-politics outlook, democratic
governance benefited. For one thing, leaders by and large
have a need to believe that their mandate to rule is legitimate.[22] We can only speculate about the strength of such
a need, or the variety of ways it can be satisfied. But to
the extent that winning an elite position, or securing the
approval of elites, could not by itself confer a sense of
legitimacy, political leaders would tend to look in another direction and seek signs of popular approbation to
confirm their mandate to rule. Again as Young has
argued:

One would infer . . . the presence of psychological stimuli in the
governing fraternity to reach out for the attention and approbation of those they govern. What better balm was there for the
democratic conscience of the rulers than popular applause?[23]

Moreover, the distrust of elites by elites helps ensure
that politics will be a basis of cleavage within elites, as
well as between them and citizens generally. Anti-power,
anti-politics attitudes, then, served as a check on the co-
hesiveness of political elites. Elite solidarity is harder to
maintain in a climate of mutual suspicion; people try to
keep distance between themselves and others, partly in

21. Ibid., p. 60.
22. See Reinhard Bendix, *Kings or People* (Berkeley and Los Angeles:
University of California Press, 1978).
23. Young, *Community*, p. 64.

deference to their feelings of distaste, partly in deference to the dictates of prudence. So are sown seeds of conflict *within* the governing society.

This cynicism of elites about elites contributed, some suspect, to the growth of political egalitarianism. It may have acted as a brake on elite aspirations and roles or, more broadly, on the emergence of a political aristocracy.[24] The absence of feudalism in America, after all, scarcely provided a sure-fire guarantee against a later lapse into a culture of aristocracy. And one reason politics did not serve as the basis for such an aristocracy— despite the abilities and ambitions of the first two generations of political leaders—was the very prevalence of anti-power, anti-politics attitudes, shared by citizens of all stations.

The absorption of political cynicism into the political culture has proved to be abiding for a variety of reasons, one of which merits particular mention. The cynicism of political elites about political elites tends to be self-enforcing.[25] A self-enforcing process is a variant of a self-fulfilling prophecy. But it differs on one point. A self-fulfilling prophecy begins with a premise about the world which is at the outset false but which becomes in some manifest aspect correct by virtue of the consequences of commitment to this premise. The classic example, I suppose, is prejudice. A self-fulfilling prophecy starts with a false expectation, say, that blacks are shiftless and cannot hold down a steady job; and by the perversity of the prophecy's social consequences, an initially erroneous expectation may be converted into one that is approximately correct. By contrast, a self-enforcing process be-

24. Ibid., pp. 60-62.
25. For a brief commentary on the family of expectation models, including self-enforcing processes, see Thomas Schelling, *Micromotives and Macrobehavior* (New York: Norton, 1978), pp. 115-124.

gins with a presumption about others that is substantially correct—in this instance, that it is prudent to entertain a certain cynicism about people in politics—and, by virtue of attending to it, maintains its validity.

Cynicism, once established, is the sort of premise of conduct that is difficult to ignore. To the extent that others take cynicism seriously, it behooves me to take it seriously too. For the balance of advantages always favors considering the untrustworthiness of others as a live hypothesis. Where it is understood that others are not to be taken at their word, only a saint will improve his standing by assuming candor on their part or by imposing it on his. Elite distrust of elites is hard to extinguish.

Diffuse Norms

Political cynicism is one dimension of a moral model of citizen politics. It embodies a short list of political sins in democratic society—instructively, in America it is a list of elite and not mass failings—that is readily comprehensible and therefore broadly serviceable. It teaches citizens at large what to look out for and what to guard against. And only if we see it so can we make out how political cynicism differs from cynicism generally.

In ordinary usage a cynic is a person who "knows" that people who say that they act for altruistic reasons in fact act for selfish ones. A cynic is anything but surprised to discover others acting in their own interest, despite their protestation that they are acting in the interest of others. For the cynic to protest that this is wrong would make no more sense than for a physicist to protest that a stone falls. But protest is just what the politically cynical do: they complain; they critize; they may even become indignant.

That political cynicism involves a certain species of outrage is a broad hint that it is a symbolic expression of rules of right conduct. Political cynicism involves not merely a distinction between the acceptable and the unacceptable, but an insistence that the distinction makes a difference. Only if we recognize its moralistic character can we understand an otherwise baffling aspect of political cynicism. Specifically, we can grasp, if only loosely and intuitively, how it is possible for citizens to become indignant at political corruption and the like— *even though many of these very same citizens are in the habit of insisting that this is the way "politics" was, is and always will be.*

Political cynicism may be an everyman's glossary of rules of right conduct—these rules or norms, however, are by the very nature of democratic politics diffuse and indefinite. A blurring of the line between the acceptable and the unacceptable is inevitable in pluralistic politics; unavoidable or not, it may perversely serve as a mechanism of social control, on balance favoring conformity to the norms of democratic politics, or so I should like to suggest.

The practice of elite politics in democratic institutions involves as a matter of course concessions and compromises—agreeing to an amendment you dislike to pass a bill you want, supporting some appropriation for another's constituency to obtain one for your own, "watering down" legislation to get it reported out of committee, to win approval in a Senate-House conference, or to escape a presidential veto. Mutual adjustment is ubiquitous in liberal democracies.

The practice of mutual adjustment shades off gradually, and imperceptibly, into the realm of the unseemly, the inappropriate, the undesirable, the improper. Often only a hazy line separates what should and what should not be done. Perhaps as importantly, the public at large lacks a discriminating view of proper political conduct.

Ordinary citizens tend to have a weak grasp on the *practices* as well as the *principles* of democratic governance. A word or deed that falls comfortably within the realm of the acceptable to the politically aware and articulate may run a formidable risk of being judged by the ordinary citizen, should he or she learn of it, as unprincipled and unacceptable.

Moreover, the line of demarcation between the permissible and the improper is not only vaguely drawn, but unpredictably variable. The enforced sense of what is wrong changes. Practices that were once perfectly proper, or at any rate not plainly improper, may become unexpectedly and suddenly illegal (e.g., rules on campaign financing); more than one public official has found himself the target of retrospective judgment. The aggregate effects of such changes are complex, but the net effect is comparatively clear cut: the very blurriness of the distinction between the acceptable and the unacceptable may keep people in line. Most of us assume that clear and precise norms favor conformity. That is often so, but that does not gainsay the importance of *uncertainty* of punishment as a means of elite constraint in pluralist politics. Where the line setting off the unacceptable from the acceptable is strictly drawn and well known, it is not unreasonable to suggest that the dominant incentive is to approach as closely as possible to the line without incurring punishment.[26] As Goode has suggested, a clear line may be a challenge: the cleverer and more daring a person is, the stronger the pressure to press up against the limits of the acceptable. In contrast, diffuse norms—or blurred lines—obscure precisely how far one may go. The calculations become more complex and unreliable; the

26. I owe this argument to William J. Goode, *The Celebration of Heroes* (Berkeley and Los Angeles: University of California Press, 1978), pp. 33 ff.

decision to test the limits of the acceptable gets riskier. Outbreaks of popular cynicism about politicians and politics have been recurrent yet unpredictable. And the uncertain may serve as a more effective deterrent than the all too predictable.

Then, too, in a democratic society, however constituted, political leaders will sooner or later find themselves committed to a course of action that touches off public dissatisfaction. A tradition of political alienation awards a certain legitimacy to public criticism of political officials and institutions. And a tradition so diffuse as the American is appropriate to nearly any circumstance or complaint. To be sure, the detailed substance of complaint may be obscured; yet the sensation of more or less intense, if not widespread, public dissatisfaction is registered. A wave of political alienation is one way that democratic elites learn that they may have made a serious mistake.

Responsiveness

Political alienation, then, may facilitate responsiveness. As a means of communication or a way in which citizens at large may signal their dissatisfaction to political elites, perhaps the chief virtue of public alienation is its loudness. And not least because of its noisiness, an outbreak of political cynicism may serve as a stimulus for elite responsiveness.

A public mood of political cynicism, it is worth emphasizing, represents as much an opportunity as a threat to elites. Political leaders may respond to public dissatisfaction, of course, out of a mixture of motives. They may fear the prospect of political turmoil. They may be moved by an altruistic sympathy with complaints that the voice and vote of the ordinary citizen no longer count. Indeed, we could set down a long list of praiseworthy motives for elites responding when the climate of public opinion has turned sour and suspicious of politics and politicians. But the point to fix on is that problems also present political opportunities.

From this angle, discontent about government bears a certain resemblance to discontent about crime in the streets, or unemployment, or property taxes, or ghetto riots. All provide opportunities for established or aspiring elites to advance political careers by publicizing their desire and efforts to eliminate the problems the public complains of. And to the degree that a show of responsiveness may redound to the advantage of the politically influential, to those who want to stay in office as well as those who want to dislodge them from it, a tradition of political alienation tends to forestall a need for reliance on elite virture in a democratic order.

Whether a tradition of political alienation proves to be on balance noxious depends largely on the responsiveness of institutions. Most theories of democratic politics, contemporary or classical, accent the incentive that electoral competition affords for political responsiveness. Up to a certain point, I believe, we have a tolerably definite idea of what we mean by this. Responding to the political demands of active citizens cuts down the likelihood they will resort to more extreme measures to win what they want and what they believe they are entitled to. Yet to say that responsiveness checks dissensus is not to say that it serves the democratic idea. Consider the discontent after World War I. Its central tenets were nativism, anti-intellectualism, chauvinism and anti-Semitism. Plainly, challenges to the prevailing political order in America may be launched on behalf of values that are noxious to the democratic idea; they may promote prejudice, intolerance of opinion, violations of constitutional rights; or, to put the point more emphatically yet, alienation may throttle dissent itself, precisely to the degree that the political order proves itself responsive.

One further caution. There is a temptation to think of

mass discontent and elite responsiveness as though the former were stimulus and the latter response. Yet very often the grievances of the alienated are too diffusely formulated to be treated as bases for a program of action to which elites might directly respond. Moreover, even if elites sought to respond reflexively to popular criticism, it would be exceedingly difficult in the swirl of the everyday world to determine which was the most compelling criticism to attend to, which the worst wrong to right, which the wisest (or most popular) remedy to advocate. In short, our sketch of the notion of responsiveness shows elites as too passive.

Elites do not merely dampen cynicism; they also arouse it. Even when they are on the average less cynical about politics than the ordinary citizen,[27] political elites are better able to articulate discontent, to publicize and build support for their views, to fix an agenda, to translate their beliefs into action and, above all, to take advantage of circumstances to press or publicize their discontent. The speed with which a practice or an institution that previously was taken for granted can become the object of a demand for change illustrates the protean quality of dissensus. It is not just with democratic values that elites are better able to connect the abstract and the concrete.

Exhaustiveness

For Americans, America exhausts the political alternatives. On examination of their opinions, one can make out traces of an alternative political vocabulary or order. But we were ourselves witnesses to the turnabout once the question of alternatives became explicit. The standard of comparison might be an actual country or an ideal

27. For some of the most recent evidence, and a brief review of earlier studies, see Jeanne Kirkpatrick, *The New Presidential Elite* (New York: Russell Sage Foundation and The Twentieth Century Fund, 1976), pp. 168 ff.

one; in either case, large numbers of the alienated bolted, and substituted a favorable evaluation of the United States for an unfavorable one. Moreover, even the comparative handful of the politically embittered who called openly for a whole new system of government showed nearly no awareness of, let alone commitment to, an alternative political order. It is difficult to exaggerate the hold of the idea of America on the imagination of Americans.

This I take to be telling. And it may help us to understand one restraint on a dynamism of democratic politics —the rivalry of actual and ideal.

It is as though democratic societies held jousting matches between the values the political order espouses and the practices they follow. Periodically, a substantial portion of the politically vocal hold the political system up to close scrutiny, and compete to find it wanting—as judged by the core values it is officially pledged to. This comparison between what is and what should be is built into the democratic idea: it guarantees alienation.

This comparison is bound to be invidious. In a democratic politics those who closely compare what is and what should be will always conclude that the former falls short of the latter. And, in this, they will always be right. As Dahl observes:

For every system purporting to be democratic is vulnerable to the charge that it is not democratic enough, or not "really" or "fully" democratic. The charge is bound to be correct since no polity has ever been fully democratized.[28]

Worse, no polity was *or ever will be* fully democratized, if only because democratic politics involves a plurality of

28. Robert A. Dahl, *After the Revolution* (New Haven: Yale University Press, 1970), p. 4.

values, which conflict under various conditions and to varying degrees, and so cannot all be realized equally and fully.

Democratic theorists have attached some importance to this process of invidious comparison, particularly in an attempt to understand better the special character of change and uncertainty in a democratic polity. It is for this reason that Dahl declares democracy "has always been and is now potentially a *revolutionary* doctrine."[29] And Sartori sees in this invidious comparison a source of irritation, easily inflamed, which always carries with it a threat of erupting into fevered contention.[30]

What makes the American experience distinctive, I would like to suggest, is the degree to which what is and what should be are identified one with the other. The two are bound up together, leaving little room for a competitive schema. Accordingly, there is little incentive to advance, and less reason to accept, rival images of a political order.

The actual is the ideal, or a very close approximation of it, in the mind of the average American. To the extent that Americans can arrive at some definite and persuasive image of the ideal, it is as though they used the actual as a mirror; even when they inveigh against established institutions, their preferences are reflected in the official creed of these very institutions. So we run into an irony of American pluralism. Although American culture is in many aspects diverse, it is in one aspect unvarying: it neither conceives nor harbors competitive conceptions of the political order. When Americans survey the way things are, they cannot discern any prominent image of a rival polity.

29. Ibid., p. 4.
30. Giovanni Sartori, *Democratic Theory* (New York: Praeger, 1975).

There is no alternative polity for the alienated to embrace. They could not imagine a political order apart from the American. When they were free to voice their thoughts in their own words, it is plain they looked upon other countries as variations on, and not alternatives to, America. America remains the promised land; perhaps more accurately, for the alienated no other has displaced it as the promised land. With only a few exceptions, even the disaffected could not bring themselves to *say* that they could leave here and live elsewhere. To conceive such an ideal, and talk about it, they spoke of permanent emigration as a permanent "masquerade" or a permanent "vacation."

Should all this appear obvious, perhaps a reminder is in order that we stand in danger of overlooking an even more obvious point: the alienated, and above all the disaffected, were patently and unequivocally alienated. By any reasonable measure, they were not posturing. The disaffected are politically embittered. They saw themselves, and were seen by others, as set on a fundamental critique of America. Some had a more ambitious or idiosyncratic conception of their mission than others; but they did represent a current of the time. And in the years shortly before we met and interviewed them, a substantial number of the disaffected had contested the authority of the political order itself, and by acts and not just words.

It would be too glib to suggest that the quarrel of the alienated is not with the provisions but the observance of the regnant principles, though to say that it is too glib is not to say that it is altogether false. But there is no competitive conception of a political order which stands out. And so there is no inviting or enduring alternative for the politically discontent to rally about.

There is an eagerness to announce bad tidings. Our

times are unsettled. There has been uncertainty and risk before, but that will not discourage those who warn of a crisis of confidence. And this preoccupation with a loss of confidence, with alienation and cynicism, centers in the end on a question of loyalty.

The test of loyalty has been allegiance, understood to mean a readiness to favor, praise, approve of or support established political institutions and practices. But loyalty need have little to do with liking or disliking government. No one had a more favorable attitude toward it than the committed but they surely were not on that count the most loyal. And the disenchanted had the habits of mind, including a balanced view of government, which equip a citizen to take part in a democratic politics. The alienated may be loyal, and the allegiant need not be.

A loss of public confidence in government can do damage, but America has periodically endured outbreaks of political disillusion and disorder—and sometimes has profited from them. To the degree that citizens are free to think or act as they choose, there is an irreducible uncertainty. The real source of risk is not alienation but democracy itself.

Appendix A
A Note on the Measurement
of Political Alienation

Developing a standard measure of alienation was an aim of the project in which I participated; it was not mine. Nonetheless a comment on the measurement of alienation is called for. The questions in the checklist all concern the national government. But surely one may hold a very unfavorable attitude toward the national government—indeed, in some sense or other be alienated from it—without being alienated from the political order itself. And so we run head on into the so-called problem of objects.

On its face, knowing *from what* a person is alienated seems terribly important. As Keniston has pointed out, an individual may be alienated from himself but not his siblings, from his family but not his peers, from his job but not his culture, and so on.[1] Perhaps the most ambitious attempt to deal with this problem of objects is the taxonomy proposed by Easton. He distinguishes three classes of "object": authorities, regime and community. It is patently one thing if a person is alienated from authorities, that is, from those who occupy the institutionalized offices of command, but it is quite another if he is alien-

1. Kenneth Keniston, *The Uncommitted* (New York: Harcourt, Brace and World, 1965); see especially pp. 449-496.

ated from the regime, that is, from "the structure and norms governing the use of their power."[2]

Apart from acknowledging the potential relevance of these distinctions, it is not clear what one can usefully say. Perhaps a good beginning is to be straightforward in advertising the price, if not the merit, of this insight that a person may be alienated from more than one thing. Apparently we need more than one measure of alienation. We cannot make do with the particular one we happen to have, *whatever one that happens to be*. As for the specific measure at hand here, the adjective checklist, it purports to be a measure of attitudes toward the national government. It was not devised, nor is it promoted, as a direct measure of attitudes toward other, more "basic" objects, for example, the political regime or the political community.

As a rule the best way to find out about something is to ask about it; the present case is one of the few exceptions. Some of what we most want to learn about is hardest to learn about *directly*. Example: the political system. Political scientists would like to know what citizens think about the larger political system, quite apart from how they feel about a certain level of government. But how shall we assess public attitudes toward "the political system"? Is it really obvious that the best course is to invest most of our resources in a direct attempt to measure how people feel about the political system? How many citizens, if asked about "the political system," are likely to have anything more than the most rudimentary idea of what so abstract and unfamiliar a notion might mean? When citizens may voice their opinions at length and in detail, as our respondents could in the extended interviews we conducted, it becomes painfully plain that by far the

2. David Easton, *A Systems Analysis of Political Life* (New York: Wiley, 1965), p. 293.

largest number, even of the rather small number who
suppose themselves to know the term's meaning, are ut-
terly at sea—an observation that will surprise few students of public opinion. On the whole, it seems improba-
ble that citizens at large carry about in their mental
baggage a proper package of ideas about such exotic
constructs as the political system. By contrast, the national government is concrete rather than abstract, familiar rather than arcane. People talk about it, think about
it, feel strongly about it, hold definite opinions about it.

There is also the so-called system-incumbent distinction. This version of the problem of objects is methodo-
logical rather than theoretical. The nub of the problem
can be briefly put: How sure are we that this measure of
alienation, or indeed any other, "measures alienation from
the political regime rather than mere disapproval of incumbent political leaders?"[3] Those raising this question
conceptually, and attempting to explore it empirically,
have performed a useful service. But perhaps a word on
this distinction is appropriate.

The issue is validity: Does a measure of political cynicism or alienation measure what it is supposed to measure? How might we answer such a question? To judge
from current research, one approach is to determine the
relationship, if any, between the respondents' political
cynicism and their evaluations of the incumbent president's performance, their party identification, their presidential vote and their "affect" toward candidates and
selected groups. When Citrin examined the Michigan
Trust in Government Index, he discovered a discomfiting
pattern of correlations: on every count the "outs" tended
to be more cynical or alienated than the "ins." In 1964

3. Jack Citrin, "Comment," *American Political Science Review* (September
1974), 68 (1974): 973-988, p. 974; see also Miller's reply to Citrin: Arthur H.
Miller, "Rejoinder," *American Political Science Review* 68 (1974): 989-1001.

and 1968, when a Democrat was in the White House, strong Republicans were more likely to be politically cynical than strong Democrats; in 1970 and 1972, when a Republican was president, strong Democrats were more likely to be politically cynical than strong Republicans. From findings such as these—and he examined a good many others—Citrin concluded that the Trust in Government Index "fails to discriminate between the politically alienated and those who mistrust particular leaders or politicians as a class without repudiating regime values or institutions."[4]

The system-incumbent distinction, which forms the core of Citrin's criticism, has a beguiling appeal. Surely in the study of alienation we do not want merely to measure whether citizens dislike incumbent officeholders. But unfortunately this line of criticism manages to transform the genuinely complex into the spuriously simple. To ask if a measure is valid is to ask if it measures what it is supposed to measure. But validity is not an all-or-nothing proposition. No measure measures only what it is supposed to measure. We go to great lengths to devise estimates of error not to discover whether a measure is error free—for none is—but to determine whether the degree of error is unacceptably large *for the particular purpose at hand*. The decision to use a measure, such as the Trust Index, rests on a host of considerations—the questions raised, the population studied and the like. If we reject the Trust Index merely because it is contaminated (to some unknown degree) by error—and this is what the argument amounts to—we should similarly reject *all* measures of attitude, preference and behavioral self-respect currently in use. By failing to specify an acceptable margin of error, this line of criticism gives itself away as a form of polemical utopianism.

4. Citrin, "Comment," p. 976.

Appendix B
Description of Indexes

Liberalism-Conservatism Index

Five items, enumerated below, were used to measure ideology.

How about the courts—some people think the courts are too easy on people who break the law while others think the courts are too hard. In your view, are the courts too easy, too hard, or about right in the way they enforce the law?

***   *Too hard*

**   *About right; other; can't say; no answer; too hard on some, too easy on others*

*   *Too easy*

On the whole, do you think the police around here treat almost everyone fairly, or do they treat some kinds of people unfairly?

***   *Treat some kinds of people unfairly*

**   *Other; can't say; no answer*

*   *Treat almost everyone fairly*

Some people believe that the authorities are too hard on people who oppose our system of government while others believe that they are too easy. What is your opinion—are the authorities too hard, too easy or acting about as they should with people who oppose our system of government?

***   *Too hard*
**   *Just about right; other; can't say; no answer*
*   *Too easy*

The poor are poor because the American way of life
doesn't give all people an equal chance.

***   *Agree strongly; agree somewhat*
**   *Can't say; no answer*
*   *Disagree strongly; disagree somewhat*

In politics, would you say that you are a radical, a liberal, a conservative, a strong conservative, or would you
call yourself middle-of-the-road?

*   *Strong conservative*
*   *Conservative*
**   *Middle of the road*
***   *Liberal*
***   *Radical*

Note: * = scored Conservative; ** = scored Neutral; and *** =
scored Liberal. The five collapsed items were summed to form an
index with scores ranging from 0 to 10; this distribution of raw scores
was collapsed into a 5-point version as follows:

	Score
Strong liberal	0-1
Liberal	2-3
Middle of the road	4-6
Conservative	7-8
Strong conservative	9-10

Verbal Awareness

To measure verbal IQ we asked people to match a target word with its meaning. Reproduced below is the exact wording of the question.

We would like to know something about how people go about guessing words they do not know. On this card are listed some words. You may know some of them and you may not know quite a few of them.

On each line there is a word in capital letters—like BEAST. Then there are five other words. Tell me the number of the word that comes closest to the meaning of the word in capital letters. If the word in capital letters is BEAST, you would say "4" since "animal" comes closer to "beast" than any of the other words. If you wish, I will read the words to you. These words are difficult for almost everyone—give me your best guess if you're not sure of the answer.

IF NECESSARY: Can you see the words all right or would you like me to read them to you?

[BEAST]	[1 a star]	[2 school]	[3 tree]	[4 animal]	[5 rock]
BROADEN	1 efface	2 make level	3 elapse	4 embroider	5 widen
ACCUSTOM	1 disappoint	2 customary	3 encounter	4 get used to	5 business
EDIBLE	1 auspicious	2 eligible	3 fit to eat	4 sagacious	5 able to speak
PACT	1 puissance	2 remonstrate	3 agreement	4 skillet	5 pressure
ANIMOSITY	1 hatred	2 animation	3 disobedience	4 diversity	5 friendship
EMANATE	1 rival	2 come	3 prominent	4 free	5 populate

Political Knowledge

To measure knowledge of politics, we asked the following questions, adding up the number of right answers.

The following questions are about American politics. Many people aren't sure of the correct answers, but we are interested in their best guesses. If you think you know the answer, check the appropriate box. If not, just check "Don't know."

How many terms can an individual serve as president of the United States?

☐	☐	☐	☐	☐	☐
1	*2*	*3*	*4*	*No limit*	*Don't know*

Not counting Social Security payments, the federal budget is about 160 billion dollars a year. About what percent of this money would you say goes for defense?

☐	☐	☐	☐	☐	☐
Less than 20%	*20-30%*	*30-40%*	*40-50%*	*More than 50%*	*Don't know*

About what percent goes for foreign aid?

☐	☐	☐	☐	☐	☐
Less than 1%	*2-6%*	*7-13%*	*14-21%*	*More than 22%*	*Don't know*

How long is the term of office for a United States senator?

☐	☐	☐	☐	☐	☐
2 Years	*4 Years*	*6 Years*	*8 Years*	*10 Years*	*Don't know*

How many of the amendments to the U.S. Constitution are known as the "Bill of Rights"?

☐   ☐   ☐   ☐   ☐   ☐
0   *1*   *5*   *10*   *22*   *Don't*
Amen.   *Amen.*   *Amen.*   *Amen.*   *Amen.*   *know*

In the last five or six presidential elections about what percent of black voters would you say probably voted Republican?

☐   ☐   ☐   ☐   ☐   ☐
Less   *15-*   *41-*   *60-*   *More*   *Don't*
than   *40%*   *59%*   *84%*   *than*   *know*
15%   *85%*

How about the following people, what is your best guess about what each one does?

Henry Kissinger	☐ *Writer for Playboy*	☐ *Mathematician*	☐ *Presidential adviser*	☐ *Author*	☐ *Don't know*
Garrick Utley	☐ *Congressman*	☐ *TV newsman*	☐ *Air Force general*	☐ *Businessman*	☐ *Don't know*
William Fulbright	☐ *Republican leader*	☐ *Newspaper columnist*	☐ *Surgeon general*	☐ *Senator*	☐ *Don't know*
Tom Eagleton	☐ *Congressman from Delaware*	☐ *Senator from Missouri*	☐ *Senator from Montana*	☐ *Author*	☐ *Don't know*
Tom Hayden	☐ *Republican leader*	☐ *Congressman from Ohio*	☐ *TV newsman*	☐ *Radical activist*	☐ *Don't know*

Index

Absorption of political cynicism, 157-161

Abuse of office, 97-98; tendency toward, 154-157. See also *Federalist*

Adjective checklist: methodology of, 16, 17 table 1, 18, 149; on quality of government, 120-121. *See also* Bay Area Survey; Mailback Survey

Adversaries and conventional participation, 84 table 19

Adversary protest, 73, 152-153; and civil disobedience, 75; and education level, 77; and range of political views, 80-83; distinguished from advocacy protest, 82-83, 102-103; participation in, by types of alienation, 88-91; and dissatisfaction, 91 fig. 3. *See also* Advocacy protest; Alienated; Disaffected; Protest

Advocacy protest, 73-76, 152-153; and civil disobedience, 75, 99; and education level, 77; and range of political views, 80-83; and restraints, 93, 95-96; efficacy of, 99-102; distinguished from adversary protest, 102-103; appeal to majority sentiments of, 100-101; routinization of, 101-103. *See also* Adversary protest; Alienated; Protest

Advocates and conventional participation, 84 table 19

Age. *See* Demographic profiles

Alienated, 7; as disaffected and disenchanted, 47-48, 54-55; judgment of, as absolutist, 58-59; feeling of powerlessness of, 61, 68; replies to comparison questions

of, 115, 119-123; proportion of, in survey, 121-123; and established order, 131; and alternatives, 169; and loyalty, 170. *See also* Disaffected; Disenchanted

Alienation, 2-5, 12, 140-141; and cynicism, 3-5; political, 6-7; and balanced judgment, 10, 87-88; and protest, 11, 86-89; as fundamental to democratic politics, 11-12, 157, 167-170; types of, 47-48; 87-88; emotional content of, 61; and protest, 88 fig. 2, 90 table 20; interpretation of indices of, 121-123; threat of, overestimated, 153; and responsiveness, 165-166; problem of measurement of, 171-174. *See also* Disaffected; Disenchanted

Allegiance, 2-4; types of, 9, 16-21; and balanced judgment, 10; idea of, 13-15; species of, 15-22, 43; aspects of, 22-26; indicators of, 23 table 2; two forms of, contrasted, 26-35; in authoritarian and democratic states, 45-46; as test of loyalty, 170. *See also* Judgment, balanced; Committed; Supportive

Allegiant, 7; as committed and supportive, 16; attitudes of, toward civil liberties, 30-33; and balanced judgment, 9-10, 16; tolerance in judgment of, 58-59; and loyalty, 170

Alternative politics, 122-123, 135, 137-141; absence from American consciousness, 168-170. *See also* America, mystique of

America, mystique of, 114, 123, 126-130, 140-141, 151, 168-170

Designer: Sandy Drooker
Compositor: U.C. Press In-House Composition
Printer: Vail-Ballou Press
Binder: Vail-Ballou Press
Text: Compset 500 Times Roman
Display: Compset 500 Times Roman Bold
Cloth: Holliston Roxite B-53548
Paper: 50 lb. Writers offset

PS

y/0111 OCP

SNIDERMAN